BELOW STAIRS

TO MY MOTHER

BELOW STAIRS

DOMESTIC SERVICE REMEMBERED
IN DUBLIN AND BEYOND
1880–1922

MONA HEARN

THE LILLIPUT PRESS

First published in 1993 by
THE LILLIPUT PRESS LTD
4 Rosemount Terrace, Arbour Hill,
Dublin 7, Ireland.

A CIP record for this
title is available from
The British Library.

ISBN   1 874675 12 0 (CASED)
1 874675 13 9 (PAPER)

Jacket design by Jarlath Hayes
Set in 10 on 12 Sabon by

mermaid turbulence

Printed in Dublin by ßetaprint

— Contents —

illustrations between pp. 90 and 91

— Introduction —

One hundred years ago domestic servants were a familiar part of everyday life in Ireland; today they have virtually disappeared. The prospect of 'managing' without a servant was unthinkable to middle-class householders in the early 1900s. Yet, within a couple of generations, that change occurred, and had a profound effect on the social life of the country. Now the domestic servant is but a fading memory to the older generations.

In the last century and the early years of this century most young girls, and some boys, from the lower social classes went straight from school to service, sometimes the very next day. They joined the ranks of what was by far the single largest occupational group for women; in 1881 48 per cent of employed women in Ireland were in the domestic class. There was a steady decrease in the number of domestic servants from then on, but domestic service was only surpassed by manufacturing industry in 1911. It was still the second largest employer of women with 125,783 female indoor servants.[1] Indeed any account of the employment of women in the nineteenth or early twentieth centuries must afford a prominent place to domestic service.

The importance of domestic service as an occupation which not only affected the whole life of those engaged in it but also impinged, in an intimate and special way, on the lives of those employing servants, has never been adequately reflected in literature, legislation, labour or social history in this country. The main reason for this neglect was probably lack of knowledge about domestic service and certainly an absence of a comprehensive view of the industry. The work place of the servant was the middle or upper-class home, and the home in Ireland and Great Britain was a private haven into which no outside interference was tolerated or indeed contemplated. Significantly, a bill: 'to regulate the hours of work, meal times and accommodation of domestic servants and

1

to provide for the periodical inspection of their kitchen and sleeping quarters' which was presented to parliament in 1911, never became law.[2] In 1918, when there was widespread disquiet about the scarcity of domestic servants, the Ministry of Reconstruction in England set up a Women's Advisory Committee on the Domestic Service Problem. The committee made certain recommendations on the organization of domestic service which were unacceptable to the Marchioness of Londonderry, who found herself unable to sign the report. She said: 'I regard any possibility of the introduction into the conditions of domestic service of the type of relations now obtaining between employers and workers in industrial life as extremely undesirable and liable to react in a disastrous manner on the whole foundation of home life.'[3]

The vast majority of Irish servants were children of small farmers, estate workers, the semi-skilled and the unskilled. The girls, unlike the daughters of the middle and upper-classes, were expected to earn their living until they got married. The lack of alternative employment in Ireland meant that they had a very limited choice; in fact the choice facing them was usually service or emigration. Those who emigrated very often entered service in their adoptive country. Because service was usually the only choice available it became the traditional haven for women from rural Ireland and from many towns and cities. This in turn added its own momentum, so that positions as servants were sought automatically without consideration of alternatives which might, in some cases, particularly at the end of the period, have in fact existed, in factories, shops or offices. Mothers and fathers anxiously looked for 'situations' for their daughters, and to a lesser extent for their sons, as the time for leaving school approached. Help was sought from neighbours, shopkeepers, teachers, clergy and roundsmen, someone was bound to know someone who was looking for 'a little girl to help with the housework'. These first places were often poorly paid but were regarded as an opportunity to learn and perhaps save a little money for the uniform needed for 'gentlemen's places'. One former servant who left school at eleven years of age, went to work for a farmer to mind a child who had a cleft palate. She was treated as one of the family, called the farmer and his wife 'daddy and mammy', but got no pay. She then went to another farm near home where she had board and lodging and 'they dressed her', but she had no regular wage; she

2

got 'a couple of pounds now and again'. It was only after these two experiences that she got a 'proper job' as a scullery maid in a 'big' house in County Meath.[4]

Domestic service appealed to parents, especially as a career for daughters, as it offered board and lodging as well as wages, and was an easy way to make the transition from father's house to the world of work. It was also acceptable to the ideology of the time which considered the home – albeit someone else's home – the natural place for a girl or woman: the work was what any woman would do in her own home. It was also the obvious destiny for those without families of their own – those from orphanages, industrial schools and reformatories. Finally, a fate, approved by parents and endorsed by society, was accepted by girls, over much of the period, as their natural role in life. Having accepted service, most girls were prepared to be happy and contented with their lot.

Taking up a 'situation' as it was called for an indoor servant was a more traumatic step than taking up a position in most other industries. It involved a complete break with home, friends and a familiar way of life; it entailed living in a dependent and subordinate position in the home of people who were not only strangers, but who were also of a different social class with different habits, values and lifestyle. Many humorous stories are told to illustrate the difficulties experienced by mistresses when untrained girls were exposed to a way of life of which they were totally ignorant. There are few accounts which highlight how harrowing and bewildering an experience this must have been for young girls. Former servants said that they were very lonely; one, from the country, said that in her first place in Dublin she 'cried for a week'.[5] The Women's Advisory Committee reported that young girls under sixteen years of age should not enter service because 'it is unsuitable for a girl to live in other people's houses, as she has not reached the age at which she is capable of readily adapting herself to new conditions'.[6]

The employer's household embraced the servants' whole life. Absolute loyalty to master and mistress was expected. Apart from some limited free time, the servant was always available to see to the wants and comfort of his employer. The total control of servant by master, which was in fact reinforced by legislation, meant that the domestic servant had little discretion over the day-to-day conduct of his life. To what extent domestic servants may have adopted the outlook and values of their employers and may have become estranged from those of their own social class is a fascinating question but one which is extremely difficult to answer. It is one of the reasons sometimes advanced to explain why trade unionism failed in its efforts to attract domestic servants. Samuel and Sarah Adams, who had worked as servants for fifty years, in their book *The Complete Servant*, advised young servants that:

as their mode of living will be greatly altered, if not wholly changed, so must be their minds and manners. They should endeavour to discard every low habit and way of thinking, if such they have; and as there will be set before them, by those of superior rank, and cultivated understanding, the best modes of conduct and the most approved behaviour, they will wisely take advantage of the opportunity which Providence fortunately presents to them to cultivate their minds and improve their principles.[7]

The usefulness of the experience gained by domestic servants in helping them afterwards to run their own homes is often given as an advantage of domestic service. The contrary view is also expressed, namely that the style and standard of living in the employer's house made it difficult for the domestic servant to adjust to the harsh reality of a working-class home and, perhaps, a subsistence wage.

Only a minority of servants in Ireland worked in country houses, yet this world has shaped our image of life below stairs. The reality for the vast majority of servants was very different. Country houses, however, provided the model for the staffing of much more humble homes. The dress, duties, conditions of service and treatment of servants in these houses were adapted by the middle classes to suit their own more modest households, and elements were clearly discernible even in the one-servant home.

— One —

MASTERS AND SERVANTS

Employers ranged from the nobility and gentry employing up to nineteen or twenty servants, to members of the lower middle classes who had that 'little girl' to help with the housework. By far the largest number of employers had one general servant. A typical example was C.L. Doyle who was a sorting clerk in the GPO in 1911. He lived with his wife and two sons in a small house, 157 St Helen's Terrace, Clonliffe Road. He was forty-eight years of age and was earning approximately £146 a year. He and his wife kept a boarder which gave him a higher income and he was able to employ a young girl aged eighteen from County Meath.[1] Most of Mr Doyle's neighbours could not afford a servant and in fact a colleague of his, James Blake, also a sorting clerk, living ten doors away at number 167, had no servant.[2] He had a family of eight children and could obviously not afford to rear a large family and keep a servant. A government report in 1899 on the wages of domestic servants drew attention to this: 'the larger the family, the less can the head afford to pay until some of the younger members become self-supporting'.[3] Charles Booth, a sociologist who investigated the life of the poor about the turn of the century, also found that less affluent homes with few members were more likely to have servants than larger households.[4]

A minimum salary of about £150 a year was required to afford a servant.[5] In 1912 a select committee of the commons investigated the wages and conditions of employment of post-office clerks in Ireland; the clerks earned between £104 and £114 a year and were described by the committee as having 'a moderate standard of living'. The annual cost of rent, food and fuel for a clerk's family in an Irish provincial town was reckoned to be £103.10.0–£108.10.0. Those advocating higher wages pointed out that this did not allow for the education of children. Neither they nor the committee mentioned the employment of a servant;[6] it was taken for granted that this was not an expense occurred by those earning £110–£120 a year. When it is considered that keeping a servant cost at least £25 a year, it is evident that an income of £150 was necessary before a family could afford one. This meant that a skilled man who earned about a £100 a year could not employ a servant; national teachers could not afford a servant, neither could a policeman. Of course some people with very low incomes hired a young girl at a small wage and made savings by reducing the quantity and quality of the food supplied.

Many people, especially from the lower classes, earning much more than £150 a year, and some with earnings from boarders and financial help available from other working family members did not have servants. While a certain income was necessary before a servant could be employed, if this was available, the middle class was much more likely to have a servant than the lower middle class. Social class, which was determined mainly by the position and salary of the head of household, was the single most important factor affecting the employment of servants. Upper-class and most middle-class families had servants; at this period the style of living of these classes required the employment of servants. An article in *The Irish Homestead* in 1915 discussed the responsibilities of a middle-class man earning £400 a year. These were seen as:

obligation to live in a better house, provide domestic help, clothe wife and children, as well as the wage earner himself according to the standard of his social status: educate (sometimes prolonged and expensively) his children, pay higher rates and taxes, and altogether incur a greater lease of life responsibilities than may fairly be said to be incurred by the average manual workers.[7]

Wives and daughters of the better off members of society were not expected to do their own housekeeping; daughters were usually not taught housekeeping skills but they were expected – it is not clear how – to acquire the ability to 'manage' servants. A former mistress said that when she got married in 1913, at the age of twenty-eight, she was totally unable to train a maid as she knew nothing about housekeeping. When she went to a registry office to interview a maid she was so ignorant about the procedure that the servant, probably taking pity on her, told her the questions she should be asking.[8]

In Dublin in 1911 98 per cent of the upper-class, most of the middle class (71 per cent) and 23 per cent of the lower middle class had servants. The two lowest classes, the semi-skilled and the unskilled, did not generally keep servants.[9]

TABLE 1

Percentage of different social classes employing one and more servants in 1911 (number of employers in brackets)

STATUS	NUMBER OF SERVANTS EMPLOYED							
	1	2	3	4	5	6	7–10	TOTAL
UPPER	21	32	19	12	7	6	3	100
	(52)	(81)	(48)	(29)	(18)	(15)	(9)	(252)
MIDDLE	68	27	5					100
	(109)	(43)	(8)	(1)				(161)
LOWER	93	5	1	1				100
MIDDLE	(73)	(4)	(1)	(1)				(79)

Source: 'Domestic Servants in Dublin.'

As might be expected, the higher the social class the more servants employed. Some of the higher professional class, living for example in Merrion and Fitzwilliam Squares, had large staffs of six or seven servants. Mr Justice John Ross, then a high court judge, who lived with his wife and grown-up daughter at 66 Fitzwilliam Square in 1911, had six servants: a butler, footman, cook, two housemaids and a chauffeur.[10] Sir Charles Cameron, who in 1911 was medical superintendent officer of health and held other public health positions for which he was paid £1000 a year, lived at 51 Pembroke Road, and employed four servant.[11]

The middle and upper-classes lived in large houses and this increased their need for servants. Houses in 1911 were often poorly planned and were usually devoid of labour-saving appliances. The style of living of the upper-classes was elaborate and friends were entertained lavishly: this standard of living was absolutely dependent on the availability of servants. Thus these people usually employed servants as a matter of course, they may have debated about the number of servants they should have, but that was the only consideration: servants were a requirement of their station in life. If they had children, they employed more servants, generally specialist servants such as nursery maids, nurses and governesses.

On the other hand, the employment of a servant by the lower middle class and indeed some of the middle class was in response to a need – such as help with children. Members of the lower middle class were more likely to have a servant if they had a young family – the number having a servant at all was, of course, low. A young girl was employed to mind the children or do the housework and help with the children. If the family was large, they did not have a servant, the older children looked after the younger ones. In the nineteenth and early twentieth centuries many families had adult female relations living with them; women rarely had a home of their own until they married or perhaps inherited their parents' home. In lower middle-class homes these women, if they did not work outside the home, obviously helped with the housework and made the employment of servants unnecessary. The middle and upper-classes tended to have more dependent female relatives, they were, after all, better able to support and house them, but these women were not expected to help in the home: their presence did not affect the employment of servants at all, except perhaps, to add to the work.

On the whole, the keeping of servants was linked to customary practice and need rather than show. As with any other possession however, servants were sometimes used for the ostentatious display of wealth and standing: more servants than were needed were employed, men were engaged rather than women, foreign servants were hired as personal servants. Elizabeth Smith, who lived in Wicklow in the middle of the nineteenth century, when deciding which luxuries she could do without, said: 'upper servants, fancied wants, indolent habits, can all be dispensed with and no great happiness sacrificed'.[12] Most employers, however, regarded servants not as a luxury or a status symbol, but as essential for their comfort and the proper organization of their homes. Even when servants posed problems for employers, or when they became difficult to obtain, the possibility of doing without servants was rarely entertained.

The majority of the servant-keeping class in Dublin in 1911 was Protestant (Protestants represented only a quarter of the general population at that time).[13] The reason for this was that positions in the public service, the professions, banking, and business were held by Protestants to a far greater extent than their number warranted.[14] These were the people who lived in the fashionable squares in the city and in the newly developed suburbs and who could afford to employ servants. C.S. Andrews, describing the development of Terenure in 1910 when he went to live there, said that the rows and squares of new semi-detached houses were occupied mainly by Protestants, employees of the big city firms; people who played bowls and tennis in Eaton Square and hockey or rugby in the local sports centre.[15] Louie Bennett, who worked for nearly forty years for the Irish Women Workers' Union, described a family who lived beside them in Temple Road in her youth as misfits. 'The Murphys were not only in business [by this she meant retailing, not 'big' business which was considered respectable], they were Roman Catholics ... and were not accepted without question within the fold of Temple Road.'[16]

Servants reflected the needs and preferences of their employers. The majority of them were young single women working in houses where only one servant was employed. They were usually called general servants, and during the 1880s the name 'thorough servant' was used in Ireland.[17] These young women were responsible, with the help of the housewife, for all the work of the house. Probably about 80 per cent of the 12,322 indoor servants in Dublin in 1911 were working in one-servant households.[18] The general servant was the only one for whom Mrs Beeton had any sympathy, describing her life as 'solitary' and her work as 'never done'. She had to do all the work which in larger establishments was undertaken by a number of servants. 'Her mistress's commands are the measure of the maid-of-all-work's duties.'[19]

Kate Ivory and Ellen Quillan were typical general servants working in Grosvenor Square, Rathmines, in 1911. Kate was employed by Mr Henry Kelly and his wife. Kelly was a commercial clerk working in a brass foundry, he had one six-year-old child; he and his wife kept a boarder. Kate was twenty-nine, single, born in Co. Wexford, a Catholic working in a Protestant household. Number 89 was a two-storey red-brick house, with the usual hall, sitting-room, dining-room and, extending away to the back, a gloomy kitchen, scullery and pantry where Kate spent most of her working life and indeed all her evenings. Across the square, Ellen, a twenty-five-year-old single Catholic from Co. Fermanagh, worked for an older couple, Mr and Mrs Robert Daly, who lived with their three teenage children at number 54.[20] Robert Daly, a member of the Church of Ireland, was a civil servant in the telegraph department of the GPO. Number 54 was larger than 89, with twelve granite steps leading to the front door. There was a door under these steps into the kitchen premises. This was the entrance used by Ellen, and the one to which the delivery men came. Ellen had to climb the stairs each time the front door bell rang, and she had to carry all the meals up the stairs to the dining room on the first floor. These two young women had to clean the houses including scrubbing the twelve steps, flagged or tiled kitchen floors and back passages. They had to light ranges and fires, carry hot water upstairs, empty slops, mind children, cook and serve meals. Kate had to attend to the needs of a boarder as well as the family.

There were many other young women like Kate and Ellen who worked alone in similar houses in the quiet roads and squares of the city. In 1911 these exclusive residential areas were indeed peaceful, with very little traffic, most of which was horse drawn. In the morning maids might be seen cleaning door brasses or, with their striped cotton dresses protected by sacking, scrubbing the stone steps leading to the front doors. Later, hard-hatted and dark-suited masters descended these steps on their way to offices and businesses in the city. During the day the quiet was occasionally broken by children going or coming from school, uniformed nurses pushing commodious prams as they took their young charges for their daily outing, and delivery boys on bicycles with laden baskets of goods from the main city shops. Indeed these boys and van men probably provided the only break in the dull daily routine for the Kates and Ellens 'below stairs' in fashionable Dublin.

When two servants were employed in these houses, one was usually a cook, the other, whose job it was to clean the house and to serve meals, was usually called general servant, housemaid or house/parlourmaid, or given no specific title. A cook was not always employed as many mistresses preferred to do the cooking themselves – at least for the main meal – and leave the rest of the housework to the servants. A number of houses had a general servant and a nurse for the children. In this type of household the employment of a second servant was only temporary and as soon as the children became older, only one servant was kept.

'With three servants – cook, parlourmaid and housemaid – a household is complete in all its functions. All else is only a development of this theme.' In larger households, the cook had an assistant, a kitchen-maid or perhaps a second assistant, a scullery maid; the parlourmaid's duties were taken over by the butler, and the housemaid had the assistance of other housemaids who might be called upper and lower housemaids. A nurse for the children might have got help from an under-nurse and nursemaids. Valets and ladies' maids were only found in wealthy households.[21] The staff structure in houses with three or more servants in Dublin seemed to have followed this pattern. The usual three servants employed were a cook, parlourmaid and housemaid. In almost one third of three-servant houses one servant was a children's nurse. What C.S. Andrews called the 'Catholic middle middle class' – general medical practitioners, shopkeepers 'who did not live over their shop', civil servants, journalists and bank managers – usually had three servants 'referred to as the cook, the maid and the nurse'.[22]

There were very few male indoor servants in Ireland in 1911. Out of a total of 1040 servants in Dublin houses only 66 were male. This was close to the percentage for the whole country in the census of that year, 93 per cent of servants were women and only 7 per cent men.[23] Even though there was a 28 per cent drop in indoor male servants between 1891 and 1911, men servants were comparatively rare even twenty years previously.[24] Men were more likely to be employed in households with a comparatively large staff of six or more servants. It was more expensive to employ men, their wages were generally higher and they ate more. When Elizabeth Smith decided to economize she declared: 'we have resolved to do without a man servant'.[25] The cost of male servants was further increased by a tax on them which was introduced by Lord North in 1777 to help to pay for the American War. It was one guinea a year for each servant at the beginning but it was gradually increased, and a sliding scale used whereby a higher tax was paid on a second or subsequent male servant. In 1799 the tax on twenty-one male servants in Castletown House was £23.17.9.[26] In 1786 a duty on hair powder affected those whose servants wore powdered wigs. An attempt was made to tax female servants but this caused such an outcry that it was abolished. The tax on male servants was reduced substantially during the nineteenth century but it was still a disincentive to the employment of men. It was finally abolished in Great Britain in 1937.[27]

Men servants were not as adaptable as women. As they were usually employed in houses where a number of staff was kept, they tended to have specialized functions. They may also have been less amenable than women to standing in for fellow servants or doing chores which they considered not part of their normal duties. Charles Booth certainly thought so; he maintained that it was want of adaptability on the part of men rather than high wages which led to the gradual disappearance of male servants from all but the most wealthy households.[28]

Of course the reduction in male servants was not due only to employers' decisions to hire women rather than men. When domestic service began to lose its attraction men were the first to move into other employment. The specialized functions that male servants usually performed prepared them for other occupations; a groom could become a public coachman, a butler or footman could become a barman, or run his own public house. The fact that they were used to taking responsibility made the transition from one occupation to another easier. Many men took jobs as non-residential outdoor servants – gardeners, grooms and coachmen, while women tended to remain as indoor servants.[29]

Domestic servants had a higher level of literacy than the general population. In 1911 92 per cent of indoor servants were literate as against 88 per cent of the latter.[30] It is clear that employers took great care when choosing a servant, therefore it is reasonable to expect that they looked for literate people. Households where a large number of staff was employed, and more specialized staff, had more literate servants. Of course the literacy rate of servants improved greatly over the thirty years from 1881 to 1911, it was only 61 per cent in 1881.[31] Many servants in the more lowly positions were not able to read and write. For this reason some kitchen ranges had the alphabet incorporated in the design on the roasting tin rest which was under the oven door, so that kitchen and scullery maids could learn their letters in their idle moments.[32]

Servants' religion was important to most employers.[33] Catholics tended to have Catholic servants and one third of servants employed by Protestants were members of their own Church.[34] It must be remembered that it was far easier to recruit Catholic than Protestant staff, 80 per cent of the general population in Dublin city being Catholic.[35] In the selection of nurses, nursemaids and companions, employers showed a definite preference for their co-religionists. As a Protestant employer said, she was happy to employ Catholic servants, but liked a Protestant nurse who could tell Bible stories to the children when putting them to bed.[36] The larger houses in Dublin tended to have more Protestant servants: a high proportion of the owners were themselves Protestants, they had more British servants, and they had more male servants, many of whom were Protestants.[37] While the religious affiliation of their servants was important to many employers, former servants did not appear to have suffered from religious discrimination. They did not feel that they had been excluded from situations on account of their religion, and they had not experienced any difficulty in practising their religion. Roman Catholicism was considered the religion of the servant class. George Tyrrell, who was later to attain fame as a leader of the Modernist heresy in the Roman Catholic Church, was brought up in Dublin in a Church of Ireland family. He mentioned childhood holidays in Skerries where:

There was the tawdry little Roman chapel in the village ... and I wondered to see gentle folk belonging to such a vulgar religion, suited only for servants. That Romanism was the religion of the Helots and of vulgar and uneducated classes in Ireland was one of the strongest, if the least rational, prejudices of my childhood.[38]

The Catholic Church of the Three Patrons in Rathgar was known as the 'servants' church'; it is reputed to have been built by the pennies of the servants who attended the church and who worked in the mainly Protestant households in that upper-class area of the city.

Domestic service was an occupation for young people and the old family retainer was probably a rarer phenomenon than her appearance in literature suggests. In 1911 47 per cent of indoor female servants in Ireland were under 25.[39]

TABLE 2

Percentage of female indoor servants in different age groups in 1911 compared with the general female population in brackets

AGE GROUP	15–19	20–4	25–44	45–64	65 & OVER	TOTAL
	24 (13)	23 (12)	35 (38)	12 (22)	6 (15)	100

Source: Census of Ireland 1911

The age structure of servants in the three censuses from 1881 to 1901 also show that servants were predominantly young. The large proportion of young servants was, no doubt, due to the fact that virtually all female servants – and possibly some male servants – left service on marriage. Employers preferred to engage young servants. This can be seen in newspaper advertisements, for example in *The Freeman's Journal* on 22 January 1889 mistresses sought: 'Respectable girl, general servant, £1 per quarter', 'Girl about 16 mind children and housework £4', 'Smart girl as general servant £6', 'Smart tidy little girl about 13 to mind children 13/- a quarter'. While employers were offering higher wages in *The Irish Times* on 1 July 1909, they still looked for young servants: 'Young General Foxrock, good plain cook, small washing, small family, £14', 'Smart Young General – plain cook, no washing, early riser, £12–£14, 80 Leinster Rd'. Young servants could be paid less, were presumed to be more amenable to new routines and surroundings, to be stronger and have more energy and be far removed from the problems that an ageing servant could create for an employer.

The majority of servants were single, they either married comparatively late and left service, or they did not marry at all. That employers preferred unmarried servants is clear from newspaper advertisements which often either stipulated that an applicant must be single or asked for a declaration of marital status. It is also clear from the apologetic tone of advertisements from married applicants who hastened to assure employers of the usefulness of their spouses to look after the garden or help with the housekeeping; childlessness was seen as an advantage.[40] In Dublin in 1911 only 2 per cent of female servants were married and 6 per cent were widowed.[41] When the marital status of female servants is compared to that of women in the general population it is clear that at any age female servants were less likely to be married than their peers. Approximately half of the female population between the ages of twenty-five and thirty-four were married, compared with only 3 per cent of servants.[42] The percentage of married male servants in Dublin (22 per cent) was comparatively high. However, most male servants worked in large houses where there was more likely to be accommodation for married servants. They usually held positions of authority or ones for which employers would prefer mature men; the majority were butlers, coachmen or chauffeurs.[43] Many would not take jobs unless married quarters were available and the type of accommodation, gate lodges and living quarters over stables and garages was more suitable for men than women.

Conditions of service and the attitude of employers did not facilitate the meeting of the sexes in circumstances conducive to courtship and marriage. Servants worked long hours with very little freedom, they had limited opportunities to meet each other.[44] This was especially true of those working in one- or two-servant households, which included the majority of servants. These girls tended to marry milkmen, breadmen, butchers, roundsmen, or small shopkeepers, probably the only men they met regularly. Marriage was looked on by many servants as a way of escaping from service.[45]

The process of acquiring a spouse was actively discouraged by many masters and mistresses. The disparaging term 'follower' was used to describe a servant's boyfriend; it was the subject of jokes and cartoons, and a 'no followers' rule pertained in many households.[46] It was even mentioned by some employers when advertising for servants.[47] Servants were thus further isolated from their own social class. The low status of their occupation also made it harder for them to acquire an eligible young man. A number of former servants said that they pretended to boyfriends that they worked in factories.[48]

Servants may also have postponed marrying until they had accumulated a nest egg which gave them greater independence and security when setting up home.[49] Certainly many Irish servants were in a position to save and they may have acquired some of their employers' middle-class values of thrift and prudence. The tendency of Irish servants to delay marriage extended to Irish women immigrants who became servants in the United States. Many of them never married. 'To work a lifetime in an employer's family without marrying was an accepted custom on the Emerald Isle.'[50]

The question might be asked whether single women found a livelihood in domestic service or whether servants tended not to marry. The latter seems more likely. Pressure, which might have been exerted on single girls living at home on farms or indeed in towns to marry and start a home of their own was, of course, lacking. At a time when match-making was common, there was no evidence that marriages were arranged for servants by their families. Some women may have entered service when they were older and not likely to marry, but the number was probably small. The difficulties of older women entering service are obvious; apart

15

from the preference of employers for young servants, older women would have found it harder to accept training and the lack of freedom and subservient role that service imposed. There was an influx of older women into service but they were widows. They were probably domestic servants before marriage and merely returned to the job for which they were trained.

Domestic service was the cause of considerable migration. Of the servants working in the Dublin houses in 1911, only 28 per cent were born in Dublin city or county: the majority had not come from too far afield.[51] In her book *Dublin, the Deposed Capital* Mary Daly has pointed out that servants tended to come from rural areas and added significantly to the number of migrants in the Dublin suburbs.[52] The main reason why most domestic servants worked a distance from their birthplace was the unavailability of work at home and the great demand for servants in cities and large towns.[53] Only a quarter of the servants in large houses in Dublin were from the locality.[54] People in smaller houses, employing only one or two young servants, tended to recruit them locally through friends, tradesmen, teachers and clergy.

The relationship between master and servant was of the utmost importance in an employment where the servant not only worked, but lived, under the master's roof. It depended primarily on the character and personality of the master and to a certain extent, on the attitude of the servant. The relationship between master and servant during the late nineteenth and early twentieth centuries was not helped by the fact that the philosophy underlying this relationship was often ambiguous. In earlier times it was based on a paternalistic system under which servants were paid low wages but were supplied with all the necessities of life, the master's house was their home and their welfare in sickness as well as health was the concern of their master. During the nineteenth century, with the growth in industralization, the work relationship in factory and office affected domestic service. In America service was modified by the growth in professional management and the emphasis on efficiency. Theoretically the work relationship of the factory should be introduced into the home.[55] Under this commercial system the master–servant relationship was governed by a contract which could be terminated on either side by a short notice, what a contemporary observer described as: 'a harsh business transaction in which one has paid as little as possible, and the other has only rendered strictly prescribed services, the master has come to regard his responsibilities at an end when the wages are paid'.[56] 'What has been lost in devotion and long service must be made up in efficiency of work', as a journalist put it in 1903.[57]

Difficulties between masters and servants during this time were often blamed on the advent of the commercial system. There was nostalgic regret for the old 'paternal' relationship. It was advocated in the 1920s that the home help should become a member of the family and give the service that is only given for love: 'this is really what the real old-fashioned servant used to do in those households where she was seen in all her glory'.[58] Undoubtedly some servants lost privileges without gaining better wages or more clearly defined working hours. In the past a certain consideration was necessary in the treatment of servants 'in order to secure, through their fidelity, affection and esteem – what we now expect from them in return for money.'[59] Of course the existence of paternalism did not rule out the exploitation of servants. The fault, however, was not in the commercial system itself – though rights and duties of employers and employees under this system, or indeed any system, were never clearly defined – it was rather in the slow transition from one system to another which was never entirely effected and resulted in the co-existence of the two, with their very different underlying philosophies. The paternalistic and the commercial systems were both in evidence up to the First World War in England and France.[60] Elements of paternalism survived in the master–servant relationship in Ireland up to the 1940s.[61]

The treatment of servants in illness reflected the different philosophies held by employers. The domestic economy manuals, adhering to the paternalistic system, said that masters had a responsibility to look after their servants when they were ill. In spite of this, many employers dismissed sick servants if they felt they could replace them.[62] Many sent staff back to their families for nursing if they fell seriously ill, or alternatively, gave them notice in the knowledge that they could, if necessary, go to the workhouse.[63] In evidence to the Royal Commission on Poor Law and Relief of Distress in 1910 it was stated that domestic servants were only out of work for short periods or for illness: 'if illness creeps in the Poor Law would creep in to meet it – or charity'.[64] Elizabeth Smith of Baltiboys treated her servants harshly when they were ill. Referring to a servant who had been dismissed, she said: 'so she has left us to her extreme sorrow, but I could not put up with her health and her impertinence'.[65] Her health, or presumably ill-health, was mentioned before her impertinence. The same lady, on another occasion said; 'these sick servants in a small household don't do'.[66] Miss Gilchrist, cook for over thirty years to the Bradshaws, the upper-class family in James Plunkett's *Strumpet City*, was treated very well by her employer until she became ill and partially paralysed when she was sent to the workhouse. Mr Bradshaw explained to the priest: 'It's not that I mind her growing old ... provided she can potter around and get her work done. But what if she is incapable? We can't employ a servant to dance attendance on a servant. The thing would be absurd.'[67] Sick servants were also sent to hospital. 'To send off to the hospital any servant who falls ill or meets with an accident is, nowadays, a custom so firmly established, that householders have come to look upon it as a natural right.'[68]

Some employers did look after their sick servants. The Clonbrock Papers record the payment of doctors' fees for servants; in May 1909 wages were paid to the garden boy while he was sick in hospital.[69] Furthermore, inscriptions on headstones testify to the appreciation felt by some employers for their deceased servants:

In memory of Patrick Dempsey, long a faithful servant of Col. J.F. Forester, died 29th March 1911 aged 56 years R.I.P.

Here lies the remains of Mrs Bridget Makison who died 15th October 1830 aged 31 years. This stone was erected by Arthur Upton Esqr. to the memory of an attached and faithful servant. May she Rest in Peace. Amen.[70]

Olive Ardilaun, the wife of Sir Arthur Guinness, erected a memorial to her head gardener, 'a most devoted friend', in the garden of St Anne's outside Dublin.[71]

A very good relationship existed between some employers and their employees: many mistresses were kind and caring and genuinely interested in the welfare of their servants. This interest often continued after the servant married and left service. Letters exchanged between the Lemon family of Yew Lodge, Clontarf, and a former servant, Biddy, show that the two kept in touch for a number of years; news of marriages and deaths in the Lemon family were conveyed to the maid who in return gave information on her family.[72] Many servants were content with their lot and grateful for any kindnesses shown by their mistresses. However, the two belonged to very different classes in society and their proximity in the home generally did little to break down barriers between the classes. Employers usually emphasized the differences and reinforced the barriers by separating – as far as possible in a small house – the maid from the family. Many from the rapidly-growing middle class, very conscious of their newly gained status, took every opportunity to underline the lowly and inferior position of the servants in their households. Even young children had to be addressed as 'master' or 'miss'. Servants had to be respectful to their 'betters'. They were expected to be as unobtrusive as possible, to speak when spoken to and to remain standing in the presence of their employers. They entered and left the house by the tradesmen's entrance, they ate on their own, usually in the kitchen. If a servant accompanied her mistress when shopping, she walked a few steps behind carrying the parcels. A former mistress recalls a friend coming to visit her in the 1920s, the friend accompanied, at a respectful distance, by her maid bearing a one- pound pot of jam, the gift for the hostess.[73] Servants wore uniform, not just as a protection when working, but also as a means of distinguishing them and their particular positions on the staff.

Employers regarded servants as a class with a certain amount of suspicion and distrust. When seeking servants they tended to stress desirable personal qualities rather than ability to do the job efficiently. They sought 'respectable', 'trustworthy' or 'superior' persons. 'Smart', 'clean', 'good' and 'steady' were other adjectives frequently used alongwith 'sober' and 'abstemious'.[74] An advertisement in The Irish Times in 1907 specified a 'clean respectful' girl.[75] Employers often sought 'humble' servants: 'a strong humble girl' was required by two mistresses in the Daily Nation on 3 July 1892. A general servant was sought in The Freeman's Journal in 1892 who was 'strong, middle aged, humble and civil'.[76] A preference was often expressed for country girls – possibly because they were considered easier to manage. It must be remembered of course that employers were not just seeking an employee, they were selecting a member of their household.

In regarding servants as inferiors and in seeking ways to maintain the distance between the two social classes, employers were merely reflecting the views and attitudes of society. Even well-meaning champions of servants accused mistresses of not knowing how to treat their 'inferiors'. When it became known in 1910, on the publication of his will, that A.J. Munby, a barrister, had married his servant in 1873, it 'caused a sensation in England and was reported in every newspaper.'[77] Derek Hudson, Munby's biographer, described Munby as a man 'ahead of his time in crossing the barriers of sex discrimination and class distinction'.[78] Yet it is clear from Munby's diaries that this 'enlightened' man was painfully conscious of the social gap which existed between employer and servant. He felt that Hannah, his servant, and himself should not be seen together; he described returning home with her: 'she would not take my arm for it was still daylight and many people were about – but walked apart till we got down into the empty streets ...'[79] In the 1870s a lady in Wales called Rose Mary Crawshay started an experiment in which she trained higher class women as upper servants. The idea of ladies becoming servants appalled many people. They said they could not bear to employ these ladies because it would hurt their own feelings to see them in such positions, a view which was commended by Mrs Crawshay. It is quite clear that this plan was not motivated by democratic ideals. Mrs Crawshay simply felt that ladies were so superior to servants that they could do the job much more efficiently:

owing to their superior intelligence, ladies 'get through' work much faster than ordinary servants: and, owing to the delicacy and refinement of ladies, they make none of the 'dirt' servants are so famed for producing. There is much less wear and tear of carpets and floorcloths by the feet of young ladies, as compared with those of ordinary housemaids.

She also made it quite clear that her gentlewomen were to be employed only as upper servants, and all the dirtier and rougher work must be done by an 'ordinary servant'.[80]

Mistresses were often accused of treating their servants as if they were machines devoid of human feelings, or, as one critic put it, 'as dumb-driven-cattle'.[81] Many blamed mistresses for the shortcomings of their servants, and it was often said that good employers made good servants. Lady Fingall said: 'Countries get the governments, and people the servants they deserve.'[82] Servants were certainly treated with a lack of sensitivity not only by masters and mistresses but by society. They were the butt of jokes, funny stories and cruel cartoons; as a contemporary said, 'the Betsy Jane of middle-class servitude does not generally tread a path bestrewn with roses. Poor Betsy Jane with her fringe and her followers – the target of many a humorous arrow'.[83] 'Oirish' servants were particularly vulnerable to this type of humour in the British press.

Former servants complained about the attitude of employers: 'generally we were looked down on'.[84] This opinion was substantiated by mistresses, who agreed that people held servants in low esteem.[85] One servant said that her master would never let 'the likes of her' into his car; in later life he became crippled and was glad to have her to help him in and out of the car and travel with him.[86] A servant who enjoyed her work said she was employed by an American whose son asked her one day to make up a foursome at tennis. She was very impressed by 'the likes of her playing tennis'.[87] In 'A Man from the Croaghs Remembers' by Patrick Campbell, 'the servant boy often felt that he was "looked down on"' by the 'comfortable farmers of Donegal' who were his masters.[88] On the other hand, many former servants enjoyed their work and did not mention their lowly status, because they accepted it as normal.

Even though, in later years, there was discussion about the need to improve the relationship between employers and their servants, very little changed. In 1920 an Irish magazine, *The Lady of the House*, discussed the desirability of having a more democratic relationship between mistress and maid. There were many letters from readers objecting to the idea: 'even the most advanced Republican believes in the monarchy of home and firmly grasps her throne as reigning queen'; and again: 'but the good old title, "mistress of the home" with all that it stands for and has stood for for generations, must be left with us'.[89]

— Two —

ENTERING SERVICE

The large number of servants and the frequency with which they changed their jobs meant that both mistresses and servants spent a lot of time and energy seeking suitable workers or situations. The simplest and most commonly used method was word of mouth. In addition to clergy, teachers, the mistress of the big house, shop-keepers and delivery men, servants also played a part in recom-mending their children, sisters and friends, indeed employers often consulted their servants when seeking a replacement or an addi-tional member of staff. Word of mouth was generally regarded as a most satisfactory arrangement in which there was no cost involved to either party, and, more importantly, the situation or servant was known to a trusted third party.

At the end of the nineteenth century and up to the 1920s, news-paper advertising was used extensively to obtain situations and recruit servants. *The Irish Times* was the most important paper for domestic service advertising and its reputation was probably strengthened by the fact that it also ran an agency for servants. In 1880 newspaper advertising was used much more by servants than by employers.[1] Newspaper advertising increased up to the 1890s and then decreased slowly at first but more rapidly after about 1916. On 14 January 1919, for instance, there were only 104 advertisements in *The Irish Times,* 20 from servants and 84 from employers: as servants became more difficult to obtain most of the advertising was done by employers.

Most of the employers who advertised were from the middle classes and wanted general servants, cooks, children's maids, housekeepers, usually described as 'working'; housemaids and par-lourmaids were next in importance. The male servants required were usually general men, hall or pantry boys, grooms and coach-men. On the other hand those looking for situations included a

22

much wider range of specializations, up to 25 different categories.[2] Upper servants used *The Irish Times* almost exclusively. *The Freeman's Journal* catered mainly for Catholics and also for servants working in one or two-servant households, lower servants and very young and inexperienced servants.[3]

Most people confined themselves to a brief statement about the situation sought or offered. Occasionally employers stipulated that the applicant must belong to a particular Church, be unmarried, or a certain age, hard-working, strong, be an early riser, have 'good discharges'; they often indicated that a servant must be flexible in his or her approach to work. Some managed to give a lot of information about the situation in a short advertisement. 'A maid to wait on elderly lady, useful in house, abstainer, I.C., needlewoman – £12 – 2 other servants'[4] and 'Wanted superior Working Help, Protestant, all cooking, housework, small family, no children; charwoman; seaside; £14'.[5] Servants stated that they were experienced, honest, had 'long discharges', no encumbrances, were hard-working, willing or unwilling to do the washing. Cooks sometimes gave their repertoire of dishes. A young girl seeking a situation as a general servant said: 'never in Dublin before; washes and makes up neatly; cooks fairly; would take instructions; be highly recommended'.[6]

Newspaper had, of course, the advantage of bringing information to a very wide public. They provided servants who were thinking of changing their job with an opportunity of considering other openings without committing themselves or paying fees to agencies. They could make direct contact with employers in their homes. Of course they could also spend a lot of time travelling and then discover that the position was unsuitable or no longer available.

Registry offices, which were widely used, developed from small shops which used to keep lists of local girls requiring situations and mistresses maids, and charged a small fee for introducing one to the other.[7] There was always a certain amount of controversy about registry offices, because some were suspected of being used for fraudulent and immoral purposes. In England, many, especially in the larger towns, had earned a doubtful reputation as resorts for prostitutes and lower grade servants.[8] Registry offices often cheated servants by charging fees which employers had already paid, demanding bribes to furnish employment, obtaining servants at lower rates to please mistresses, and misrepresenting working conditions.[9] Evidence was given to a Royal Commission on Labour in 1893 that registry offices were dishonest, that they allowed servants to put down their names and pay a fee when they could not find employment for those already on their books.[10] A select committee of the House of Lords, which in 1881 examined the law relating to the protection of young girls, found that registry offices, even if not directly involved in prostitution, could cause a lot of trouble by enticing girls to London pretending that they had jobs to offer; the disappointed and penniless girls then often turned to prostitution. The select committee was told that a proprietor of a registry office in the Paddington area was convicted of this offence.[11] Witnesses were asked if any Irish girls had been brought over and become prostitutes; the answer was that there was no case known to them.[12]

Registry offices in Great Britain and Ireland were not licensed or controlled in any way until the twentieth century, unlike France where Louis Napoleon licensed agencies in 1852 (by 1909 there were 203 authorized agencies in Paris).[13] The Act designed to bring registries within the ambit of the law was the Public Health Amendment Act, 1907.[14] This allowed local authorities to make by-laws to control the registries, leaving to them the option to exercise regulative powers, and thus legislation was not introduced at all in many areas. Also, an agency which lost its licence in one part of the country could move to an area in which there was no control. The necessary bye-laws to regulate and licence registry offices were introduced in Dublin on 8 May 1911.[15] The act was not properly enforced. The lord lieutenant opposed the appointment of a full-time inspector of registry offices on the grounds that there was not sufficient work to justify such an appointment, and that the work could be done by the existing sanitary staff.[16] In 1911 a Miss Anna Kavanagh, who was a temporary sanitary officer, was given the responsibility for inspecting registry offices.[17] Her career as an inspector was short-lived and her services in this capacity were terminated on 30 June 1912.[18] The only report on the inspection of registry offices in the minutes of meetings of Dublin Corporation up to 1922 was in 1912 when Miss Kavanagh was acting inspector. During the first quarter of the year 6 out of 34 registered agencies were closed.[19] This should have been a cause for concern, especially when it is considered that those registries were possibly among the more reputable offices. Four of these were closed on sanitary grounds. The health committee admitted that: 'to a great extent the inspection of these offices is purely with sanitary objects'.[20] This emphasis on the sanitary rather then the fraudulent or immoral was perhaps inevitable when a sanitary officer was appointed to this position

The extent to which Irish registry offices may have been used for fraudulent and immoral purposes is difficult to ascertain. No evidence was discovered and a letter from the Regular Hotel & Club Workers' International Union to Augustine Birrell, the Chief Secretary, in 1913, stating that several cases of fraud, blackmail and withholding of original references had come to the notice of the union did not mention immoral activities.[21] Commercial registries seemed nonetheless to have been regarded with a certain amount of suspicion. The 1909 report of the Girls Friendly Society said about young girls: 'it is wiser for them to avoid strange registry offices'.[22] There were, of course, a number of well-run registry offices in Dublin and in large or medium-sized towns.

Servants considered registry offices expensive. Employers and servants paid fees. A fee of perhaps 2/6 was paid to put one's name on the books and an additional fee or a proportion of the first month's wage was paid when the client was 'suited'. Sometimes a higher fee, perhaps 5/-, was paid by mistress and maid and this covered the placement charge.[23] If a situation or servant was not obtained the fee was forfeited. Employers sometimes paid more than servants and upper servants usually cost more than lower servants, a butler perhaps 7/6 and a kitchen-maid 2/6.[24]

Registry offices provided facilities where clients could wait, separate waiting rooms for ladies and servants. Many had cubicles or rooms where interviews could be carried out, though employers often preferred to interview servants in their home. Registry offices often had accommodation where servants could stay while seeking a job. A servant without a job was also without a home: this added immeasurably to the misery and hardship of the out-of-work servant. A former servant described an apartment in Miss Doyle's agency in Holles St where she stayed as comfortable with a big flagged kitchen and a good fire. She had to supply her own food and she paid Miss Doyle when she got a job. Another servant, an orphan, stayed at 35 FitzWilliam Place, a house where domestics could live while they sought work; she paid 2/- a week.[25] Lodgings for servants run by agencies were one of the areas that the abortive Act of 1907 was supposed to control. The choice of servant or job in registry offices was limited to those available at a particular agency; this could be a big handicap especially if the registry was small. In spite of their disadvantages, registry offices were probably second in importance, after 'word of mouth', in bringing employer and servant together.

Philanthropic and religious bodies also played a part in placing girls in service. The religious in reformatories and industrial schools naturally sought work for the young people in their charge. Frank O'Connor in *An Only Child* tells how his mother who was brought up in the Good Shepherd Orphanage in Cork was placed by the nuns. One evening when she was fourteen or fifteen, the mistress of studies came to her in the workroom and told her she had found 'a nice home for her with two ladies who had called to inquire for a maid'; she was then given the regular convent outfit for girls leaving the school – 'a black straw hat and black coat, a pair of gloves, and a parcel of clean aprons'.[26] The House of Mercy, Lower Baggot St, which ran a training school for laundresses and domestic servants, started a registry office in 1914. To help the girls pass the time while they waited to be interviewed by prospective mistresses, a retired nun ran needlework classes. In the first years an average 100 girls found situations through this registry office, the number dropped to 65 in 1919 and by 1921 only 35 girls were placed. This reflects the decrease in popularity of domestic service quite evident at that time.[27]

As part of their work in helping girls leaving national schools and going into the world, the GFS founded registry offices and homes where girls could stay while waiting for situations. These offices were free for the girls but employers paid a fee.[28] In 1883 there was a GFS registry in Dublin and in four other centres.[29] Originally these offices were intended only for GFS members but membership was open to all. Members were warned that those who were placed in good service should not depend on repeated assistance. A member who declined a place or left without good reason was to have her name removed from the registry office's book.[30] It was decided in 1899 to charge members seeking other than the first place a fee of 1/-,[31] and in 1897 non-members were allowed to use the registries for a fee.[32] In that year the GSF placed 147 girls, 117 members and 30 non-members.[33]

26

In the context of the total number of servants in Ireland, the activities of the GFS in promoting and placing servants was not very important. As a means of placing Protestant girls in service and supplying Protestant servants it was probably much more significant. The membership of GFS was open to all but was used mainly by members of the Protestant Churches. A report in 1898 stated that 'the great difficulty in organizing this department throughout the country seems to be that in some parts there are so few Protestant servants'.[34] Religious bodies were popular sources of servants as employers, no doubt, trusted agencies run by the church and charitable organizations. In 1909 the GFS received 1466 applications for servants though it was only able to supply 175.[35]

Another method which merits brief mention was hiring fairs. These persisted in Ireland well into the present century and were used mainly for farm servants and, towards the end, mainly for farm workers.[36] Of course the distinction between a domestic servant and farm worker was often blurred and girls were expected to help in the house and also to look after the cows and the poultry. The report of the department of agriculture for 1906, when discussing agricultural labourers, pointed out that women were generally hired as domestic servants.[37] In 1955 a seventy-nine year-old man recalled: 'there used be servant girls at the Hiring Days too and many a farmer would prefer to get a girl than a boy, and sure they used to have to do the milking and everything too'.[38]

Many people found the idea of hiring fairs distasteful and indeed they did resemble cattle fairs and slave markets in a number of ways. Paddy the Cope described how he was hired at a fair in Strabane. He was made walk up and down so that the farmer could judge him. Paddy heard the farmer say to a friend 'he is wee, but the neck is good'.[39] In *Children of the Dead End* by Patrick MacGill, at a fair in the north of Ireland, farmers examined servants

after the manner of men who seek out the good and bad points of horses which they intend to buy. Sometimes they would speak to each other, saying that they never saw such a lousy and ragged crowd of servants in the market place before, and they did not seem to care even if we overheard them say these things.[40]

In 'Open-Air Labour Exchanges', published in the *Times Pictorial* in 1944, Michael Murphy wrote: 'some day a mature social consciousness will starve the Hiring Fair into a memory'.[41]

Before a domestic servant could hope to obtain a good situation she had to get a reference from her previous employer testifying that she was of upright character and a diligent worker. Without such a reference a servant's career was seriously threatened. Unfortunately there was no legal obligation on an employer to give his servant a 'character'.[42] Several attempts were made in the early years of the twentieth century to bring in a bill making it compulsory upon employers to give a reference to workers leaving their employment, but without success.[43] A vindictive employer could thus deprive a servant of her means of livelihood. French servants were better protected because the servant had the legal right to obtain a certificate stating the length of service and the date on which the servant left without further comment on his ability unless requested by the servant.[44]

The absolute necessity for a good reference was stressed by former servants and mistresses alike. One needed not only a good reference, but one from the last place in which one worked.[45] The GFS reports contain a note from the council urging working associates (those who placed the girls in service) to: 'lose no opportunity of impressing upon girls going into service the importance of keeping their places, remember that a character for good service is the best and surest guarantee of future employment'.[46] A seventeen year-old servant who wanted to leave her job in a Dublin hospital in the late 1930s was refused a reference by the Reverend Mother who did not want to accept the month's notice and maintained that the girl was in her charge. The girl left nonetheless and put an advertisement in *The Irish Times* to which she got eight replies. She tells how she spent the next two months walking around Dublin – up to ten miles a day – foot-sore and weary with string tied around the soles of her shoes to keep them on. In each house she was asked for her reference and got the same response: 'if the holy nuns wouldnt give you a reference you must be a very bad girl'. Luckily for her the mother and daughter who eventually employed her were willing to look for a testimonial from a nun who had been a patient in the hospital when she worked there.[47] The importance of references is seen from the fact that they were invariably mentioned in newspaper advertisements seeking both servants and situations. An employer seeking 'a respectable, steady Woman to take charge of two children' added 'none need apply only those who have the best of references'. A young girl from the country looking for a situation as a housemaid or general servant described herself as 'one whose character can bear the strictest investigation and can be highly recommended.'[48]

'In giving a Character, it is scarcely necessary to say that the mistress should be guided by a sense of strict justice. It is not fair for one lady to recommend to another a servant she would not keep herself.'[49] In spite of Mrs Beeton's strictures this was a common practice and had necessitated, as early as 1792, the introduction of an act which decreed that anyone giving a false character to a servant, knowing it to be false, could be fined £20 with 10/- costs. A similar penalty was imposed on a servant who presented a counterfeited character.[50] Servants did forge references, which is not surprising when it is considered how vital they were to a servant's career.[51] In 1902, 1903 and 1904 attempts were made to introduce a false character bill, but it never got beyond the first reading.[52] The practice of giving misleading references continued. In *Good Behaviour* by Molly Keane the nannie is sacked 'but given quite a good reference with no mention of her drinking; that would have been too unkind and unnecessary, since she promised to reform'.[53] Whilst employers sometimes erred on the side of leniency when writing references for charitable, if misguided, reasons, servants could unjustly be given poor references.[54] An unjust reference was only actionable if a servant could prove that the employer had acted with malice, a very difficult thing to do.[55] Employers generally checked servants' references by getting in touch with former mistresses.[56]

Servants had another grievance: references were held by employers and servants had to ask for them when they were leaving. Employers were, of course, obliged to return references.[57] Registries could also retain original written references belonging to servants; the trade union wanted this practice banned in the bye-laws for registries introduced in 1911.[58] Servants felt very vulnerable when documents essential to the furtherance of their careers were in the hands of others.

It is quite understandable that employers should have insisted on good references when employing servants. They were not only hiring a worker, they were taking a stranger into their home and family. What was reprehensible was the lack of control and safeguards, especially for servants, which existed in an area which was crucial to the employment process.

Very few servants received any formal training before entering service, the only instruction they got before they sought their first place was that gained at home. The number who received sufficient instruction at home to allow them to take paid domestic work was probably insignificant.[59] In fact, the difference between the standard of living in their own home – usually subsistence – and the comfortable, if not luxurious standard in the employer's home would have come as a revelation to young servants. Others got some experience in poorly paid jobs near home,[60] in what were known as 'petty places' in England.[61] As late as 1940 the Report on Vocational Organization stated that domestic service 'was still a matter of apprenticeship'.[62] This was also true in Britain and other countries. The vast majority of servants were trained by their mistresses or by upper servants.[63] An 1899 government report had stated that: 'The absence of any system of training for general servants is a serious defect in our social organisation. At present the good servant, like the good mistress, is unfortunately born not made, and is consequently rare'. The same report stated that: 'at the top, the want of a "professional" training alone disqualifies the most efficient general servants for promotion to the households employing many servants and paying higher wages'.[64] What was called 'the lag in the educational system' was blamed for the lack of formal training in England and France.[65] However, formal training for domestic service was not a success in the United States, and it was considered by many there that the only successful training was done on the job.[66]

This method of training had a number of disadvantages. Many people felt that mistresses could not teach their servants something about which they were ignorant themselves.[67] Mrs Beeton's book, *Household Management*, and similar manuals were designed to help mistresses in the task of training and organizing domestic staff. Even if mistresses had the necessary knowledge and skills, the likelihood of the servant receiving a systematic training was not high. *The Irish Homestead* in 1902 gave 'Practical hints on the training of servants as cooks' in which it was pointed out that not every mistress had the leisure or strength to train servants and spoke of 'the utter absence of any system or method in the training of the average domestic servant'.[68] Any training which a mistress gave a servant was designed to expedite the performance of the domestic chores in her household according to her wishes, as one servant put it: 'most mistresses trained girls in their way of doing things'.[69] This was not necessarily the best way, neither was it always useful in other situations. The training given by upper servants was probably more satisfactory. Firstly, the upper servant at least knew how to do the job herself; secondly, on account of the specialization in these households, the content of the job could be more easily defined and presumably, taught. Also, the training was usually more systematic and extended over a number of years. Finally, households in which a large staff was employed were usually organized in a manner that was widely accepted, and servants trained in one house could move easily to another similar house. The Report of the domestic service sub-committee on training of 1919, while conceding the value of this training, pointed out that it is probably limited to

technical instruction in the branch of domestic service selected, since for the most part, the upper servant herself is not possessed of more than technical knowledge, and is quite unable to explain the reasons for the various processes which have been adopted as a result of experience. Hence the intellect is not trained and the domestic servant tends to become mechanical in her work and her intelligence suffers in consequence.[70]

The formal education system in Ireland provided little of what could be considered training for domestic service. The development of technical education really only started with the passing of the 1899 Technical Instruction Act,[71] a similar act of ten years earlier had not been a success.[72] Progress under the 1899 Act was slow, and the main work in both urban and rural centres was done at evening classes. In the county schemes instruction was usually given by 'itinerant teachers' on short courses of five evenings a week for approximately six weeks. *The Irish Homestead* in 1902 and 1903 reported that four-month courses in cookery, laundry and sick nursing were held in places like Glencar, Creevela and Killorglin.[73] These were intended for farmers' daughters and were primarily meant to help them run their own homes. In 1902 four hundred girls and women attended evening classes in Kevin Street Technical School – courses included shorthand, typing, bookkeeping, French and German, cookery and dressmaking – eleven of those were servants. This is a very small number and many may not have been attending cookery classes; on the other hand 218 had no avowed business or profession and some of these may have been acquiring knowledge of cookery with the

31

intention of seeking work as servants.[74] 'Thirty lessons in the year in either cooking or laundry work cannot be called training' as was pointed out in *The Irish Homestead*.[75] However, such courses could give a limited foundation or enhance already acquired skills. Even by 1924, the main work of the schools was the provision of evening classes.[76] Therefore the number of girls who had access to full-time courses was limited, and many who could avail of them did not do so. The Report on Vocational Organization stated that

in recent years facilities are afforded in continuation and technical schools for learning the rudiments of housewifery, but until technical certificates command a reasonable minimum wage there is not sufficient inducement for girls to spend time and energy obtaining them.[77]

Comparatively few girls took these courses and there is no evidence to suggest that they were ever considered adequate training for service. All those advocating formal training had something more specialized in mind. A member of the Irish Women Workers' Union, in evidence to the Commission on Vocational Organization in 1940, suggested that residential hostels should be set up in every town for training indoor domestic servants. When asked if this was not being done by the vocational schools, the witness said that those schools could teach cookeery and laundry work but only in a residential hostel could girls learn the full work of a house.[78] Obviously it was felt that schools for training domestic servants should be residential or at least have access to residential facilities.

There were six residential domestic economy schools in Ireland run by religious in places such as Carrick-on-Suir and Drishane.[79] They were intended to teach household skills, poultry and dairy work to farmers' daughters. The training would, of course, have been suitable for domestic servants and, no doubt, some did take up that occupation.

The Castlerosse Training School was one of the few schools set up specifically to train servants and it had a much longer life span than most of the others. It was founded by Lady Castlerosse in Killarney in 1900, in the demesne of Killarney House, one door opening into the park, the other into the street of the town. The house was described as 'bright and cheerful, and dainty in its simple good taste'. The school could accommodate twenty-two boarders and the same number of externs; the boarders paid 4/6 a week and the externs £1 per quarter. These fees in addition to revenue from what was described as a 'needlework industry' and a laundry attached to the school financed the undertaking. Some girls who wished to know how to manage their own homes were also accepted.

A manageress, who was trained in Kildare Street, was in charge of the trainee domestic servants. She superintended the girls, showed them how to do their work and gave lectures and demonstrations in domestic economy. The timetable was:

Monday	Cookery and housewifery, 10am to 12.45pm
	Cookery and demonstration, 2 to 3pm – Practice, 3 to 4pm
Tuesday	Cookery and housewifery, 10am to 12.45pm
	Scullery work, 2 to 4pm
Wednesday	Cookery and housewifery, 10am to 12.45pm
	Cookery demonstration, 2 to 3pm – Practice, 3 to 4pm
Thursday	Coodery and housewifery, 10am to 12pm
	Needlework, 2 to 4pm (Girls' own work.)
Friday	Cookery and housewifery, 10am to 12.45pm
	Lecture on domestic economy, 2 to 4pm
	Laundry every day in the week from 9am to 12.45pm and 2 to 6.30pm

The training of a housemaid lasted not less than nine months and, if possible, one year. She was taught to clean the living rooms of the girls, to practise on the bedrooms of the matron and needlework teacher and the drawing-room, which were furnished like those in any private house. Parlourmaids received the same length of training, they were taught how to clean silver, lay a table and wait on the manageress and the other girls. Those who wished to become cooks learned plain and high-class cookery and practised by cooking for the household. Every Friday afternoon the matron gave a lecture on Domestic Economy. 'Thus when they leave the school they will have an idea of the cost of things, of how to make the best use of everything, and a certain knowledge of accounts.' Girls were obliged to keep themselves neat and tidy; at class, they wore print dresses and clean aprons. In the evening they amused themselves as they chose, reading, playing games and perhaps dancing, and at Christmas they had a party and were allowed to invite friends.

At the end of the course girls who had proved satisfactory were provided with suitable situations. It was the policy of the school to train girls to work in Ireland, not to go abroad. 'It aims at fitting Irish girls to earn in Ireland the money which is so often given

to English people and foreigners, and not to enable them to swell
the stream which is draining the life of the country.' By 1903 a
considerable number of girls had already secured excellent situations and the manager found it impossible to supply even half the
applications made to her for servants.[80] By 1911–12 the
Castlerosse Training School had forty-five students, twenty of
whom got situations at wages of £14–£18. The school was still
training approximately twenty servants a year in the 1930s.[81]

The Kildare Street Dublin School of Cookery, Laundrywork &
Dressmaking was established in the early 1890s by the Royal Irish
Association for Promoting the Training and Employment of Women, and for a few years it was possible for girls to get special
training in housewifery there.[82] However, in August 1903 it became the school for training domestic economy teachers under the
control of the Department of Agriculture & Technical Instruction.[83] In 1905 a school of housewifery was started in Saint Kevin's
Park, Kilmacud, in conjunction with a holiday home for Catholic
women workers of limited means. An instructress was appointed
by the benefactor to train the girls either to run their own homes
or to work as domestic servants, the women on holidays were
used to give practical experience to the girls.[84] Again, this school
was taken over by the DATI in 1909 when teacher training was
moved from Kildare Street to Kilmacud.[85]

The House of Mercy, Lower Baggot Street, was started in 1831
'for the training and employment of poor girls of good character
as laundresses and domestic servants'.[86] The school could accommodate forty girls, all of whom were over fourteen (most were
between sixteen and twenty on admission). They stayed until they
were ready to take up a job and this varied from a few months to
up to three years. Some came from orphanages and industrial
schools where managers failed to place them at sixteen and were
unable to keep them any longer, others were country girls who
wished to train as domestic servants. All had to be recommended
to the nuns as being of good character; many were vouched for by
religious. The nuns did not get any government grants, but
depended on bequests and donations to run the home.[87] Between
1880 and 1920 the average number of girls in the school was
twenty-six, 358 went into service, an average of nine per year.[88]

The Church of Ireland opened a training school for Protestant
girls in 1906, the Domestic Training Institute for Protestant Girls

in Charlemont Street, Dublin. It was under the board of the general synod and was recognized by the DATI. It was primarily intended for girls holding county council scolarships but was also open to others for whom a fee of £15 was charged for the year's training. The GFS offered a scholarship to the institute, however, very few Protestant girls applied for the scholarships, showing their lack of interest in service. In 1908 fifty scholarships were available but only three were awarded to Protestants, not because they were refused to them but rather because they did not apply.[89] This school had a comparatively short existence; by 1912 it was in difficulties caused by heavy costs, rent, taxes, salaries and the falling off of public support.[90]

Training for domestic service was provided in workhouses, industrial schools and reformatories. Even though the number trained was not large – less than 400 girls annually – these institutions were important. They were one of the few places providing formal training for domestic servants: the inspector of reformatories and industrial schools in 1880 highlighted this when he said: 'farmers, even with large farms, complain that industrial school children receive a training and instruction in trades which their sons and daughters cannot hope to obtain'.[91] Domestic service was the main outlet for girls from these institutions and was the 'trade' referred to by the farmers. Workhouses, reformatories and industrial schools were seen as an important source of servants by the farmers and townspeople living in their vicinity. The extent and quality of the training provided varied over time, from one type of institution to another and between individual institutions of the same kind. Wherever industrial training for girls was given, however, it was directed mainly towards service.

There was a lot of criticism of the training given in workhouses. In the early 1850s there were unsatisfactory reports from New South Wales and South Australia on the suitability of girls from Irish workhouses as domestic servants; they were described as 'generally well conducted, but ignorant of the domestic work for which they were principally required'.[92] As a result of this it was suggested that pauper girls could be boarded out

under the care of cottagers where they would be taught how to run a house and would be overseen by an 'association of ladies'. In this way girls would receive a more suitable training for domestic work than could be given in a large impersonal institution.[93]

This point is also stressed by Florence Davenport-Hill in her book *Children of the State*. She said that even when girls helped with the household tasks in workhouses it did not teach them anything of the arrangements of a well-ordered household. The girls were often a hindrance rather than a help, unacquainted with the names and uses of kitchen articles: 'the intricacies of such arts as cooking, needlework, bread-making, etc., are not instinctively perceived'. She quoted the report of the local government board for 1880–1 that

though praiseworthy efforts are made in the large unions to develop this side of education, there is a certain absence of system in many cases, which renders the instruction desultory, and therefore almost worthless. The haphazard and irregular way in which, in small unions, the so-called industrial training is conducted, imparts a degree of slovenliness to their work which operates very prejudicially when the children are first sent out to service.[94]

Florence Davenport-Hill stated that one of the reasons why the system was so unsatisfactory was that it was almost entirely run by men, she urged placing the girls 'under a discreet but firm matron'. It was pointed out that, while eternally proclaiming 'home' to be the only sphere of a woman, state-educated female children were given no idea of what a home was. They did not get affection, care or responsibility for household duties. The author stressed that the provision of industrial training in workhouses was made more difficult due to what she described as 'communication with and contamination from the adults'. Girls might be trained as nursemaids but this would constitute a danger by bringing them into close contact with numerous unmarried mothers. She thought that there had been a general improvement in the care being taken to choose the girl's first place and to supervise her work; but was critical that the law only required that a girl should be visited in her first place, after that the girl was entirely on her own.[95]

The report of the Poor Law and Lunacy Inquiry Commission in 1879 gave interesting information on the industrial training of children in workhouses. Information was obtained from the clerk of each Poor Law union. A study of the replies from forty unions showed that the industrial training of the girls generally consisted of learning to sew and knit, mend their own clothes and do washing. Occasionally housework was mentioned, which seemed to consist of scrubbing floors, cleaning dormitories etc. The industrial work was supervised generally by the schoolmistress, occasionally by a matron. In Clonmel Union girls got some experience in the infirmary kitchen and in the masters' and matron's kitchens. In the South Dublin Union girls were employed by the female and married officers and were trained as domestic servants. In Cork a special superintendent had been employed to train girls and domestic appliances had been purchased. However, the number of girls of a suitable age fell and the superintendent had to be dismissed. Since then the schoolmistress taught the girls sewing, knitting, washing, scouring and cooking.

It would seem, from these accounts, that criticism of the training for domestic service given in workhouses was well-founded. Workhouse kitchens were not suitable for teaching cookery as the work there consisted of cooking a limited range of foods in very large quantities usually using steam. Only in a very few instances was an effort made to provide training under circumstances which might approximate to conditions in a private home. The Cork Union, one of the largest, which did make an effort, had to abandon the plan because there were not enough girls to justify it.

In their replies the clerks of the unions stated that the guardians had no difficulty placing children in service, and that the demand far exceeded the supply. An exception was Macroom where it was said that: 'there was difficulty in putting them out to service as a very few of them gave satisfaction'. In Mallow there were fewer applications as the guardians had made a rule that an employer must have a valuation of £30 or more. The ages at which children were placed varied from ten to fourteen (the usual age being twelve to fourteen). About half the clerks said that children generally retained their first place; five stated the opposite and many did not answer the question, possibly because they did not know the answer. The reply from Cork was: 'From the general imperfection of their training and habits as servants, they do not in most cases retain the situations they first obtain. They are re-engaged, however, from time to time, the intervals being principally spent in the Workhouse.' The Ballymoney report said that, while the boys retained their first places, the girls did not give as much satisfaction 'in fact as servants they are a failure'.[96] In its appraisal of industrial training and placements the same report stated that

The defect of workhouse education appears to be the want of systematic, well-organised industrial training. Too much is sacrificed to merely literary advancement. As there are some unions in which industrial training is carefully attended to, and with the best results, why should it not be insisted upon in all?[97]

In 1880 the local government board of Ireland sent a general circular to inspectors of workhouses regarding the education and training of children. In this it was stated that girls should be taught to knit and sew and be involved in the ordinary work of the household, scouring, cleaning, washing and ironing, to prepare them for becoming good servants.[98] Cookery was not specifically mentioned, or methods which might have overcome some of the unsuitability of institutional-type experiences which had been criticized.

The 1887 Report of the Local Government Board also expressed dissatisfaction with the industrial training of girls. It stated that: 'of 2363 girls, 1879 are taught sewing and knitting and only 104 employed in laundry or other work which might fit them for domestic service'. The board said that if industrial training was not satisfactorily provided in future the board of guardians and union officers would have to explain their omission.[99] In 1892 the local government board's annual report gave favourable mention to the district school in Trim that catered for workhouses in Drogheda, Dunshaughlin, Kells, Navan and Trim. Forty-nine girls were receiving instruction in sewing, knitting, washing, cooking and general housework. There was a dressmaker and a cook-cum-laundress employed in the school in addition to a matron and three schoolmistresses.[100] A Royal Commission on the Poor Law in 1909 recommended that all children from workhouses who were hired out to service should be supervised for some time afterwards and that guardians should be empowered to retain the supervision of children up to the age of twenty-one.[101]

With the introduction of industrial schools in 1858 there were fewer children found in workhouses: the number of children under fifteen in workhouses fell from 18,099 in February 1864 to 9184 in 1884 and 5988 on the 31 December 1899.[102] Training for girls in industrial schools was always much more satisfactory than in workhouses. This is not surprising when it is considered that industrial schools were set up for a limited group of people, children between the age of six and sixteen, usually girls or boys who were committed for specific reasons, and were not, like the unions, catering for the destitute poor of all ages and both sexes. Children who were found begging or homeless, orphans, children whose parents were in prison or were drunkards and could no longer control them, or those who frequented the company of thieves or prostitutes could be committed to industrial schools. These schools were smaller, less forbidding institutions than workhouses, and were usually run by religious who had a deep interest in the children.[103]

The rules and regulations for certified industrial schools in Ireland stated that not less than six hours must be devoted daily to industrial training and not less than three to scholastic training. Industrial training for girls was to consist of 'needlework, machine work, washing, ironing, cooking and housework'. Where practical they were to get training in dairying, poultry and gardening.[104] The schools were inspected regularly and reports included information on the state of general education and industrial training, together with the details about the girls discharged during the year. The 1880 report showed that schools provided the neeedlework and household work stipulated; many stated that girls were taught the duties of housemaids or of parlour and housemaids. The inspector said that training in girls' schools had been particularly successful. The report on Booterstown Industrial School for Roman Catholic Girls, which was visited on 23 September 1879, said that some girls were transferred to the House of Mercy, Baggot Street, for training as household servants. A number of schools prepared girls for other occupations such as glove-making, shirt-making, lace and crochet work, millinery and dressmaking; some of the more able girls were prepared for teaching or to act as governesses in private families.[105]

The inspector's report in 1884 said that the teaching for girls had always been very practical, the results obtained most satisfactory, and the children obtained employment easily when they left the schools.[106] In 1899 the inspector again commented on the satisfactory nature of industrial training: 'in all the girls' schools, with very few exceptions, there has been a marked improvement in every branch of industial training this year'. Two schools got special praise, Hampton House Industrial School for Protestant Girls in Belfast, and St Michael's School for Roman Catholic Girls in Wexford. A method used in one of them, whereby six senior girls were allowed a tradesman's wage and each in turn had to act as housekeeper and cook for her 'family' of six for a month and keep an account of all expenditure, was described. 'These girls, when they leave, give the greatest satisfaction to their employers.'[107]

The inspector reported in 1905 that he had issued a syllabus to the schools' managers 'to show what is aimed at in the training of girls', and added that most of the subjects mentioned were already efficiently taught in the best of these schools.[108] For John Fagan, industrial training for girls meant training in domestic science, which he defined as 'the knowledge to make the home and its inmates healthy and happy'. 'This', declared Fagan, 'is woman's work', and 'if managers succeed in placing girls in the world capable of doing this, they will accomplish a great and good work for the poorer classes in the country.'[109] John Fagan then identified 'four essential kinds of industry' in which every child should get a good practical training – housework, needlework, laundry work and cookery, and kitchen work and housekeeping. He maintained that girls should start industrial training at thirteen when they enter first standard. At sixteen, when they left, they should have received a sound practical education which would enable them to make a respectable livelihood. The detailed syllabi for the four areas which John Fagan issued had been drawn up with the help of managers of wide experience and good records in the training of children. His aim was to establish a uniform and systematic method of training for all industrial schools.[110]

Two years later Fagan expressed satisfaction with the way in which the syllabus was implemented.

Praiseworthy efforts are being made by managers of all girls' schools to work through the courses of domestic science. The course of training in this subject which all the children have now to pass through is well adapted to qualify them for positions as intelligent, capable servants, or would enable them to manage small households on their own on sound economic and sanitary lines. The good effect of the training which the children now receive is already showing itself by the increased demand on the schools for good servants ...[111]

The same report stated that industrial training for girls in two reformatories, in High Park, Dublin, and in Limerick, was very satisfactory and that there was steady demand for girls trained in these schools for domestic servants.[112]

In 1914 the inspector pointed out that there were still a few girls' schools where the requirements of the domestic science syllabus were not fully carried out.[113] In reports on various schools it is seen that the industrial training of girls was judged, to a large extent, on the implementation of the domestic science syllabus. These reports included information on the staff which showed that experts such as dressmakers, cooks and laundresses were employed to train the girls.[114] The inspector's report in 1920 stated that the industrial training given in the schools was on the whole satisfactory.

This special training of the girls in domestic science enables them to fill good situations in private families. Numerous applications are received by managers every other day for such servants. The reports received from ladies who have employed these girls either as cooks, laundry maids, nurses or housemaids are generally of a satisfactory nature.[115]

Reports on the inspection of schools gave details of the specific jobs of those who were placed in service; a large number were general servants, some were laundrymaids, kitchen-maids, housemaids, cooks etc. Records kept by the schools also gave that type of information; again most girls were placed as general servants. This shows that in these schools girls were prepared for different positions within domestic service. In workhouses, on the other hand, only the most basic general training was given.

To ascertain the contribution that industrial schools and reformatories might have made to domestic service in terms of the number of girls entering the occupation annually from these sources, every tenth report was examined from 1879 to 1920. Taking 1879, 1889, 1899, 1909 and 1918 as examples, the average number placed in employment or service from industrial schools was 382. The number from reformatories was much smaller, an average of 18. The numbers dropped from 33 in 1879 to an average of 12 after 1900, probably due to more girls being referred to industrial schools rather than reformatories (Table 3). This number included all employment that girls entered, not just domestic service: the statistics do not distinguigh between service and other industries. There is no doubt, however, that the majority went into domestic service. The inspector's report for 1918, which does give that type of information, shows that of the 400 girls placed in employment from industrial schools, 329 (82 per cent) went into service. This included 49 housemaids, 11 kitchen-maids, 167 general servants, 30 laundrymaids (some of whom may have gone into public laundries), 5 dairymaids, 1 between maid, 3 scullery maids and 1 gardener.[116] It should be noted that over half the girls became general servants; this meant that most girls from institutions found employment in one-servant house-holds. They usually found employment also in the same locality as the schools; most 'situations' were arranged as a result of applications by employers to managers.[117]

TABLE 3

Number and percentage of girls discharged from industrial schools and reformatories going into 'employment or service' between 1879 and 1918

YEAR	INDUSTRIAL SCHOOLS		REFORMATORIES	
	no. to 'employment or service'	% of no. discharged	no. to 'employment or service'	% of no. discharged
1879	342	63	33	56
1889	386	55	13	50
1899	363	55		
1909	419	66	9	100
1918	400	69	15	83

Source: Reports of the inspector appointed to visit reformatory and industrial schools of Ireland.

Domestic service was of paramount importance to the schools as the occupation most likely to employ girls when they reached sixteen. At that age government grants ceased, and managers had to arrange to return the girls to the care of relatives or friends or to find employment for them. When this was done the girls were officially discharged from the institution. Most went to what was described as 'employment or service'. Why service was differentiated from other employment is not clear, perhaps it was because it also provided girls with a home or perhaps the money wages offered were too low. The next largest number returned to relatives or friends. A small number of girls emigrated and again many of these found positions as domestic servants.[118]

Managers of industrial schools and reformatories had to report to the inspector on the conduct of the children for three years after they left the schools. The reports on the girls were usually good, with approximately 90 per cent doing very well. The number who had been 'lost sight of' was comparatively small. Of those discharged from reformatories in 1876–8 (135 girls) it was reported in 1880 that 86.4 per cent were 'doing well', 3 per cent were 'doubtful', 6 per cent reconvicted and 4.5 per cent lost sight of. As might be expected, the proportion 'doing well' from industrial schools was higher; for the same years 1876–8, of the 1374 girls discharged, 92.8 per cent were making satisfactory progress.[119]

TABLE 4
Progress of girls discharged from industrial schools 1906–11[120]

YEARS	discharged	'doing well'	'doubtful'	convicted	unknown
1906–8	1740	1643 (94%)	26	1	30
1909–11	1714	1686 (98%)	18		10

The book of discharges for one of the reformatories for girls, St Joseph's Reformatory, High Park, Dublin, for the years 1880 to 1920, showed that just over 50 per cent of the 357 girls who left in that period went into service. When girls were unsatisfactory or did not improve the nuns were reluctant to place them as servants and preferred to send them home. In one instance in 1880 a girl who was described as 'most troublesome, unsatisfactory, with a light and giddy mind, and hard to control' was placed as a child's maid because she had no proper guardian; however, the sister who was worried about her kept in touch with her employer. Another girl was described as 'troublesome and not satisfactory throughout the whole time of her detention. We declined placing her in a situation and returned her to her brother.' Of another it was said that 'her conduct during her detention was not satisfactory, fearing to place her in a situation in Dublin, we have returned her to her parents.' Most girls were described as 'good and well-suited for household duties' or 'fully competent to earn a livelihood as a servant'. Some were held in high esteem, 'we could not say too much in praise of this girl'. One girl was described as 'not getting on as well as expected in her situation'. A 'well-reformed girl' was placed in service with a Mrs McDonnell in Highfield Road, Rathgar, in 1919. She was subsequently reported as 'getting on well' and it was said that her wages would be raised the following year if she continued to give satisfaction. On the whole girls were deemed suitable to work as servants and most were satisfactory at their job.[121]

Golden Bridge Industrial School was a large school which had an average of 130 pupils over the period 1880 to 1920. During that time 877 girls were discharged, 301 of whom were placed in service.[122] The nuns kept in touch with the girls for up to three years after they left and for longer in many cases. Details, not only

43

of the first situation, but also of a second or subsequent one were sometimes kept. A girl discharged in 1886 to become a general servant in Rathmines left that job in 1887 because lodgers were kept, and went to a situation in North King Street. In 1888 she was once again looking for a job; an entry in the discharge book said that as she had always been somewhat deaf it was not easy to find a place for her. A girl who went into service in 1887 is reported to be in the same situation in 1890. Maggie Hatch, who was discharged on 1 July 1886 and went to a house in Maynooth as a 'thoro servant', had to leave after six or eight months due to deafness. It was reported that 'she has changed to a humbler place where she has no bells to answer'. Mary O'Connell, who was sent home to her mother in November 1900, is reported in 1902 as doing well in a situation and her temper is described as 'greatly improved'. About a girl discharged in 1901 it was said, 'as Mary is too small and young for any kind of service, a good lady living in Dundrum has taken her to help her servant, an excellent girl who was also in this school'. Bridget McPartland who was placed as a general servant in a 'small family' in 1899 was still 'giving satisfaction' to the same employers in 1903. The girls seemed to remain in their positions as long as servants generally if not longer. This is borne out by the high 'doing well' rate reported nationally. Out of a sample of fifty-eight girls in Golden Bridge, only six received poor reports. Many of the entries show the interest and concern of the nuns for the welfare of the girls.[123]

Training for domestic service in workhouses, industrial schools and reformatories is interesting because it was the only sustained attempt in Ireland in the nineteenth and twentieth centuries to prepare girls to work in one of the principal occupations open to them. Apart from these institutions, formal training played a comparatively small part in the preparation of domestic servants for work. Yet, in spite of that, it was a subject about which much was written throughout the years. It was a constant theme of reformers in the nineteenth century,[124] it was even more common in the present century when the number of servants declined and it was seen as a method of enhancing the status of service and increasing its ability to compete with other occupations. This was stressed in the Report of Domestic Service Sub-Committee on training in 1919.[125] The increased interest in education, especially technical education, in the early twentieth century also had its effect. There were demands for certificates for servants, standardization of training and a fixed rate for the job as in other occupations.[126]

However, a satisfactory system of formal education for domestic servants never materialized, and the problem was solved by the disappearance of the domestic servant from most homes. In the USA 'the rumour that courses in home economics were training students for domestic service could kill a program', and only schools for institutional housekeepers and teachers of domestic science did well.[127] The same thing happened in Ireland and probably in most other developed countries. In 1904 Horace Plunkett complained that the establishment of a system of teaching domestic economy was 'beset with difficulties'. Apart from the lack of trained teachers there was the problem 'of making pupils and their parents understand that there are other objects in domestic training than that of qualifying for domestic service'.[128] Instead of training enhancing the status of domestic servants, the low esteem in which servants were held seems to have frustrated whatever efforts were made to provide a proper system of training.

— *Three* —

CONDITIONS OF SERVICE

Unlike other workers, money wages was only one aspect of servants' remuneration; board and lodging formed a considerable part of the real wages of servants. In addition servants often got an allowance of tea, sugar and beer; they received presents, tips and other perquisites. These factors must be considered when reckoning servants' wages and comparing them to those of workers in other occupations.

There were great variations in money wages from one household to another and from one servant to another. The wage was affected by the income level of the employer, the age and experience of the servant, the number of servants employed, the location, and supply and demand. The wage was finally a personal one – that agreed between employer and servant. When servants moved from one situation to another they invariably got higher wages. This can be attributed to their experience but it also highlights that each servant had a base line which she was not willing to go below. One servant, who was a cook in a guesthouse in Kensington and earning £40 a year in 1926, returned to Ireland in 1927 and got a situation in a private house in Shankill at £48 a year. Her employers were Americans which may help to explain what was an exceptional wage for that position in Ireland at the time, but it also shows the reluctance of servants to, as they would see it, worsen their position by accepting a lower wage.[1] This element of personal negotiation was also seen in the fact that former servants always got conditions – free time and holidays – which were at least as good as those in their former situation.

In spite of the differences which always existed a certain pattern was discernible. General servants were paid more if older, more experienced women were required. Higher wages were paid in households with larger staffs, thus housemaids, parlourmaids and

house/parlourmaids were normally paid more than general servants, who were, of course, the most common type of servant.
Children's maids and nurses were paid more than those who were
employed 'to mind the children' or 'to help in the house and with
the children'.[2] Low rates of pay were usually offered to 'young',
'young country', 'to train', or 'never-out-before' girls. Young girls
recruited from orphanages or by word of mouth through roundsmen or shopkeepers were badly paid right up to the 1920s –
wages varying from £4 to £8 a year.[3] Starting wages given to children from workhouses were approximately £2 per year. The clerk
of the Union in Clonakilty, in his report to the Poor Law and
Lunacy Inquiry in 1880, observed that 'wages are low, but quite
equal to their value'.[4] Domestic servants on farms in Ireland were
paid as little as 32/- a year in the 1870s,[5] and 50/- in 1896;[6] about
1906–10 they were paid £8–£12.[7] What were considered lower-
grade servants, especially the younger ones, were paid consistently
less than the average servant in middle- and upper-class houses.

Cooks were the second most common type of servant
employed in one- to three-servant households. There were two different rates of pay for cooks, one of approximately £18 a year,
and one of about £30. The former was paid in houses where
cooks had duties other than cooking, their wages and indeed their
job were more akin to those of a superior general servant, and
most worked in one- or two-servant households. The higher rate
was paid to cooks who had purely culinary duties; advertisements
for cooks offering £30 often mentioned that a kitchen-maid was
or was not kept, showing that such a cook might expect to have
an assistant and that a degree of specialization existed.[8]

Wages for general servants and cooks, the two most common
categories of servants, are shown on Table 5. They were taken
from *The Irish Times* and *Freeman's Journal*. The wages for general servants in the two papers were so different that they have
been shown separately. They reflect the different readerships, the
former, the upper middle-class, mainly Protestant, household with
generally two or more servants, the latter, the lower middle to
middle-class Catholic household with usually one or perhaps two
servants. On the whole, the provincial papers catered for the same
type of readership as the *FJ*. These rates of pay were consistent
with those received by former servants or recorded in the account
books of employers.

TABLE 5
Average wages of servants in 1880–1920 from advertisements in The Irish
Times *(IT) and* The Freeman's Journal *(FJ) (wage span in brackets)*

	GENERAL SERVANT		COOK (*IT*)	
YEARS	IT	FJ	'ordinary'	'superior'
1880–9	£8.3	£5.6	£13.8	£30
	(£6–£10)	(£3–£8)		
1890–9	£9.0	£7.6	£14.2	£30–£35
	(£8–£14)	(£4–£12)		
1900–9	£12.5	£9.0	£18.0	£30–£40
	(£10–£18)	(£5–£15)		
1910–20	£14.3	£14.8	£18.7	£30–£40
	(£12–£22)	(£9–£20)		

TABLE 6
Average wage paid to servants in three country houses 1880–95

WOMEN	WAGE	MEN	WAGE
cook/housekeeper	£47.50	butler	£57.0
housekeeper	£40.00	coachman	£41.0
cook	£34.00	2nd coachman	£25.0
lady's maid	£26.50	footman	£22.0
nurse	£25.00	groom	£15.5
head laundry maid	£21.00	hallboy	£9.0
head housemaid	£20.00		
kitchen-maid	£18.75		
2nd housemaid	£16.00		
dairy maid	£14.00		
2nd laundry maid	£14.00		
schoolroom maid	£13.00		
1st nursery maid	£12.50		
under housemaid	£11.50		
2nd nursery maid	£10.00		
scullery maid	£10.00		
3rd laundry maid	£10.00		
still-room maid	£9.00		

Sources: Account book: Wages. Servants' wages, 1885–92, kept by Henry Theo-
philus Clement (Clements Papers: TCD, Ms 7288). Wages Book of Domestic Servants Employed at Dromoland by Ethel, Lady Inchiquin, 1880–6 (Inchiquin Papers:
NL, Mss 14848–9). Farm, Household and Personal Account Books of Luke Gerald
Dillon, 4th Baron Clonbrock, 10 vols, 1886–1917 (Clonbrock Papers: NL, Ms
19547).

Upper servants were paid considerably more than any servants in
middle-class homes. Many cooks in country houses – who were
described as professional cooks – were paid £50 or £60 a year, the

cook in Dromoland was paid £50 a year in 1880. It is also clear that promotion was possible from, for example, under housemaid to head housemaid with a consequent rise in wages.

Wages in the homes of the nobility and gentry in Ireland seemed to be more like wages in similar establishments in England. Wages paid to servants at Englefield House, Berkshire, in 1875–91 are very similar to those paid in Dromoland Castle in 1880–6.[9] Likewise the wages suggested for upper servants by Mrs Beeton in 1906 are similar to those paid in big houses in Ireland in 1880–94.[10] This similarity is not surprising as a large proportion, especially of upper servants, were recruited in England. The lower servants, scullery maids, stillroom maids, hall boys, were usually paid less than their English counterparts. These were the positions held by Irish servants and their wage rates were determined by Irish standards which were lower than those in England.

The wages of servants increased with age up to the age of thirty-five or forty;[11] experience and presumably efficiency were rewarded by many employers. As with all aspects of domestic service there was no uniformity about this; some servants had to ask for rises which were reluctantly given or had to threaten to leave. It was fairly common to give servants a rise within the first year of service, many employers appeared to regard this period as probationary and to promise a rise if the servant proved satisfactory.[12] Indeed rises were usually given in the earlier period of a servant's working life. After the age of twenty-five to thirty in the case of general servants and housemaids, and the age of thirty to thirty-five in the case of cooks, length of service was not usually accompanied by increases in wages. Most servants reached the height of their earning power at the age of thirty-five to forty; changing positions became difficult after that and certainly servants' bargaining power diminished. It was an important reason for male servants, especially, leaving service and taking up a new career. One of the main reasons given for the rapid turnover of domestic servants was the need to change jobs in order to get a wage rise.

It was found that in Ireland wages varied directly with the number of servants in the household, the greater the number of staff the higher the wages. Miss Collet's report also showed that this happened in England and Wales.[13] Charles Booth, in his study of domestic service in London in the 1890s, found that servants' wages increased with age up to middle age, and that wages increased as the number of staff rose.[14]

Wages of servants in Ireland between 1880 and 1920 show a steady rise in the rates paid (Table 5). Great variations existed at all times but the upper limit increased. Alterations in wages are usually related to the cost of living to see whether or not there has been an improvement in buying power or 'real' wages. To a large extent servants were cushioned against rises in the cost of living as most of their expenses were paid by their employers; when the cost of living rose the value of the board and lodging element of their wages also rose. When it fell, other workers experienced a rise in 'real' wages which servants did not enjoy.

There was a rise in money wages generally of 11 per cent in the United Kingdom, including Ireland, between 1880 and 1889. At the same time the cost of living dropped by 15 per cent, giving a rise in real wages of almost 30 per cent.[15] During the same decade money wages of servants rose more slowly, the wage of a general servant by about 8 per cent, and as the value of board and accommodation decreased, the real wages of servants dropped. Between the late 1890s and 1910 the money wages of general servants and lower-paid servants rose by about 39 per cent (see above p. 48) at a time when the cost of living was rising slowly and the real wages of other workers were only rising by 5–8 per cent.[16] Money wages of higher-paid servants, for example cooks, rose more slowly than those of lower-paid servants. This is consistent with the evidence given by former upper servants; their wages in the 1920s and 1930s were not dissimilar to those in country houses in the 1880s. A butler who worked for the King-Harman family was paid £75 a year in 1934; £60–£75 was still usual at that time.[17] It must be remembered that the cost of living rose sharply, by 75 per cent, between 1914 and 1924[18], so this helped to keep servants' wages more or less comparable to those of other workers.

Servants in capital cities earned higher wages than those working in other parts of the country.[19] Miss Collet's report showed that wages in Belfast were 10/- to £2 higher than in Dublin, which, in turn, was £1 to £2 higher than in Cork and Limerick.[20] The high wages in the north can be explained by the greater availability of alternative employment. Advertisements in the provincial press showed that rates offered for general servants and 'good plain cooks' were at the lower end of the scale for general servants and cooks quoted in *The Irish Times*.[21] Capital cities generally offered a wider range of employment than the rest of the country and therefore had to rely on a supply of domestic servants from areas outside the city, Dublin was no exception. In 'Domestic Servants in Dublin', it was found that 72 per cent of servants were from outside Dublin city and county. Even though working in the capital had an attraction for many, wages had to be sufficiently high to ensure that an adequate work force was maintained. In addition, many wealthy people with large staffs lived in the city, and wages tended to be higher in such households.

Servants were usually paid quarterly, which was also usual in Britain.[22] Indeed in that country they were sometimes paid only twice yearly; a demand of a trade union founded in Dundee in 1872, was that wages should be paid every quarter instead of every six months.[23] Servants were unlike most other workers in this respect. The custom probably arose because they were not dependent, like others, on wages to buy the daily necessities of life. Perhaps that was the excuse given by many employers for paying their servants irregularly; a number of former servants mentioned that they often had to ask for their wages. The method of payment changed slowly and servants in the 1920s and 1930s were usually paid weekly or monthly.[24]

An advantage which domestic servants had over other workers – and this was because they were not unionized – was that they did not lose money on account of strikes. They were not affected either by the work stoppages of others. They also probably had more control over their own employment and suffered less from the effects of minor illnesses as they did not lose their wages at those times.

Money wages were probably much less than half the total remuneration of the servant. About 1912 the annual living costs for a girl – from the same social class as servants – was £13 if she was living at home and £21 if she was living independently in a rented room. It must be remembered that a working girl then had a mere subsistence standard of living and expenditure was equal to, or a few pence below, income.[25] All expenses, with the exception of dress, were included in the board and lodging of servants. As servants wore uniform, the cost of dress was less for them. The total wages of a general servant in Ireland earning a money wage of £8–£10, and there were many of these throughout the whole period from 1880 to 1920, was about £25 a year. In these cases, board and lodging at £13 a year, accounted for a half to two thirds of the total wage. These calculations are based on frugal living costs, but as most servants had the same food as their masters and lived in good housing, their standard of living was more akin to that of the middle class and the value of the board and lodging element of their wages was higher.

The cost to an employer of a servant's keep was usually reckoned at £15–£18 a year, but it seems probable that this was an underestimation.[26] When employers were away from home it was usual to pay board wages to servants and allow them to cater for themselves with this money. In Powerscourt in 1906, male servants were paid board wages of 11/- a week and female servants were paid 9/-;[27] the Robin Vere O'Briens paid 12/6 a week.[28] This only covered the cost of food and did not take account of expenses such as heat, light, laundry. Some employers thought it more economical to pay board wages all the time though this was not usual in this country. However, it was fairly common here to pay 'breakfast wages' of 2/6 or 3/- a week. The servant was supposed to provide her own food from this allowance, but there was little doubt, especially where breakfast wages were concerned, that it often went to supplement wages and that the servant managed to help herself from her employer's provisions.[29] Most employers probably did not know what the keep of servants cost them, and with many servants in a position to help themselves to food, the cost, no doubt, was much higher than it should have been.

In addition to money wages, servants frequently obtained presents, tips and other perquisites. The practice of giving Christmas presents was widespread – money, dress lengths or other items of uniform, cardigans, shawls or nightshirts, pipe and tobacco, books, Bible or stationery boxes.[30] Most presents were practical which was probably appropriate at a time when people found it hard to supply themselves with the necessities of life: more frivolous gifts would, perhaps, have brightened the festive season for people whose work always kept them separated from their families at Christmas. Servants received tips for performing particular services or from guests staying in their employers' homes. Tips of 2/6 and 3/- were given by members of the Vere O'Brien family to maids in the homes of their friends between 1880 and 1886.[31] This was quite high at a time when a housemaid might have earned 5/- to 8/- a week. In 1904 and 1905 the Clonbrock family gave tips of

1/-, 2/6, 3/- and 5/- to servants in houses and hotels.[32] Servants in middle-class homes could also expect some tips from visitors to recompense them for the extra work that guests created. There were other perquisites which were often considered the right of servants holding special positions, notably the cook, the house-keeper and the butler. Tradesmen were only too willing to give discounts on orders placed by these servants who might have had what was called an 'arrangement' with the shop: at the very least they usually received little gifts when settling accounts. The cook considered that she had a right to sell dripping, rabbit skins and used tea leaves; the butler felt he had a claim on candle ends and perhaps an occasional bottle of wine; These 'rights' could be, and often were abused.[33] It is impossible to put a money value on these other sources of income, but their prevalence has to remembered as an additional bonus for service.

As important, if not more important, to the servant as wages were the other conditions of service, accommodation, quality of food, free time, cost of uniform and general treatment by employ-ers. Working conditions were of paramount importance in an occupation which encompassed the whole life of the servant. There were vast differences between working as one of a large staff in the homes of the gentry, or working as a general servant in the homes of the lower middle classes. Former servants testify that great differences could also exist between conditions in house-holds of a similar kind.[34]

One of the difficulties of assessing the standards of accommo-dation and food provided is that masters and servants judged them from very different perspectives. Employers stressed repeat-edly that accommodation and food provided for servants was infi-nitely better than they were used to in their own homes. Servants, on the other hand, tended to compare their bedrooms, dining hall and food to conditions enjoyed by employers and their families. There was no such thing as a set standard for board and lodging which should be provided by employers and expected by servants. An attempt was made in 1911 to set standards when Mr Bottom-ly, MP, introduced to parliament the Domestic Servants Bill 'to regulate the hours of work, meal times and accommodation of Domestic Servants, and to provide for the periodical inspection of their kitchens and sleeping quarters'. This bill was rejected and standards for service were never prescribed.[35]

Servants usually slept in attic or top-floor bedrooms which they may have shared with one or sometimes two others. These rooms were plainly furnished with an iron bed, chest of drawers, wardrobe and perhaps a wash-hand basin. Servants in middle-class homes rarely had a sitting-room, they used the kitchen,[36] which, of course, was usually the living room in their own homes. Many servants were content with these arrangements. Mary Healy, writing about her aunt who worked as a housemaid in a big house three miles outside Kilkenny in the 1920s, was critical of the accommodation for servants. Her aunt shared a bedroom with another housemaid in the servants' wing which was in a bad state of repair. There was a curtain across one end of the room about shoulder high behind which all kinds of rubbish was stored – such as old curtains and trunks. The only redeeming feature of this room was the view from the window of the lovely garden. Later Mary herself worked in a house, which although very large, had no sitting-room for the staff; they sat on hard-backed kitchen chairs in front of a black stove and 'did not even have the luxury of looking at a flame'.[37] These criticisms show that, while facilities might be deemed adequate, no effort was made to make servants quarters comfortable or attractive.

Some servants undoubtedly had very poor sleeping accommodation. A writer in *The Irish Homestead* in 1905 drew attention to the number of times she had to speak about accommodation offered to domestic servants: 'the cupboards and black holes in which so many Irish domestics are expected to sleep are a disgrace to civilisation'.[38] A woman who worked as a general servant early in the century was put sleeping in the bathroom. She could not go to bed until everyone else had retired, when she had to open the window to leave out the steam; of course she also had to rise early before the bathroom was required.[39] Servants were probably, as employers maintained, at least as well housed as they would have been in their own homes, but that in the nineteenth and early twentieth centuries was not necessarily justification for complacency.

Food supplied to servants varied very much, depending mainly, it would seem, on the generosity of the employer. On the whole the food was good, in many cases it was the same as that eaten by the family.[40] Even if servants were given different food this did not necessarily mean that their diet was poor.[41] It was in households which really could not afford servants that shortage of food was usually experienced. In these houses food was often rationed and supplies kept in a locked cupboard.

The working hours of domestic servants is difficult to assess. If the time spent in an employer's house is considered as working hours – and many servants would have said that they were on duty from 6.30 a.m. until they retired at 10 or 11 p.m. – then the number is formidable indeed and well in excess of the working hours in any other occupation. Many people contended that servants were not working all the time; they went for messages and, depending on the type and organization of the household, had free time in the afternoon or evening.[42] Servants did not work at an even pace throughout the day, there were busy times and times when there was little or nothing to do; they could also, to an extent, work at their own pace. Most servants, however, when in their employer's house, were considered available, if required, for any chore that might arise. In this sense servants worked from fifteen to eighteen hours a day, and free time, to them, was time spent, as they thought fit, outside the master's house.

Servants' leisure varied greatly, but the usual, from at least the turn of the century, was a half day every week starting after lunch and a half day every second Sunday with a fortnight's holiday in the year.[43] In England there was an improvement around 1900 in the free time allowed to servants[44] and letters from employers to *The Lady of the House* in 1906 would seem to suggest that a similar improvement occurred in Ireland. One writer, while agreeing with other correspondents about the improvement said: 'servants have too few relaxations; their working hours and their duties are alike undefined and unlimited'.[45] This would appear to have been true, especially for general servants, right up to the final days of domestic service.

Servants' free time was not inviolable. Half-days only began when all the work after lunch was done and everything prepared for the evening meal; 'half-days' of only two and three hours were recorded. Servants mentioned having to wash up after dinner or supper when they returned from their evening out. A former servant said that her half-day could be any day which happened to suit the mistress, so she could never make plans.[46] A former kitchen-maid remembered taking the dog for a walk around Dublin on her half-day and paying the food bills.[47] Many servants had far less free time, some had no half-day,[48] others had no holidays.[49] Employers justified the lack of free time allowed by maintaining that servants would not know what to do with leisure or would use it badly.

There was genuine concern about how servants spent their free time and the lack of facilities for them. The GFS and the YWCA both provided social settings where maids could spend Sunday afternoons and their half-day during the week.[50] This provision was mainly for Protestants. There was a house at 35 FitzWilliam Place where servants who were out of work could stay and dances were held for them twice a week, Thursday and Sunday; men were not allowed to attend these dances.[51] Attendance at church services and membership of sodalities had social as well as religious significance in the life of many servants;[52] likewise servants often attended classes for the companionship they offered as well as the instruction given. Some employers were concerned about the lack of recreational facilities for servants. Lord and Lady Aberdeen, for instance, made attempts to make provisions for their own servants. These efforts were but a tiny response to an enormous problem. In 1940 the Report on Vocational Organization drew attention once again to the 'need for the provision of clubs where domestic servants can find shelter, entertainment and facilities for the useful employment of their leisure time and hostels where they can be housed during periods of unemployment'.[53]

The vast majority of domestic servants had to depend on their own resources during their free time. Those who were lucky enough to live nearby probably spent their time at home. Some former servants who worked in one- or two-servant households said that they usually spent their half-days in their attic bedrooms which were freezing in winter and too hot in summer.[54] One servant, an orphan, said she spent her half-day in bed. 'I didn't know the city and you didn't make many friends if you were an orphan.' In the summer she sometimes went to St Stephen's Green, which was nearby, and fed the ducks.[55] Generally servants seemed to spend their free time either alone, or in the company of another servant, visiting, walking around the city looking at the shops or going to the cinema, music or dance halls. One servant recalled seeing the film two or three times until it was time to go back to work,[56] of course in earlier days and in country areas there were no cinemas. Servants working in the country, who were not from the region, had to spend their free time in their employer's house or taking long walks.

It must be remembered that at the end of the nineteenth and beginning of the twentieth centuries holidays and leisure were restricted for the majority of the population; amusements and entertainments were few and reserved for special occasions. Thus the lot of domestic servants was not any worse than that of most people; where the difference occurred was that servants were living in the homes of others and their isolation and loneliness were more keenly felt in their leisure time, separated, as they were, from family and friends.

Before entering service at all, girls generally had to provide themselves with a uniform. Until about the middle of the nineteenth century women servants usually wore their own clothes with cap and apron, which was what wives and daughters wore at that time in their own homes. Then it became usual for them to wear special cotton print dresses with, of course, a cap and apron. The cost of this uniform for a girl entering service was £2–£4, which posed a problem for small tenant farmers, unskilled or semi-skilled workers.[57] Some charities helped poor girls by providing them with a complete outfit.[58] Girls from workhouses were provided with their first uniform which had to be returned if the girl left her position within six months.[59] While some servants liked the uniform, many looked on it as a badge of servitude, they resented especially having to wear a cap.[60] As uniform was used by the new middle class mainly to indicate the distance between mistress and maid, it is not surprising that servants associated uniform with their lowly position and, as they became more independent, rebelled against it.

Servants seem to have been healthier than their contemporaries in other industries. As they were better housed and better fed than a large proportion of the population, and their working conditions were better than in other industries, this is not surprising. Their death rate was low,[61] but as the majority of servants were young, that is not particularly impressive. However, when deaths from tuberculosis – one of the most common causes of death among the lower classes at that time – were examined, the statistics for domestic servants were very favourable. They came after the professional class with the second lowest death rate.[62]

The wages of domestic servants have little meaning until they are compared to wages in other industries, at least those competing for their services. One of these was the retail trade. It was usual at that time for drapers' assistants, and indeed assistants in grocery and general stores, to live in, either over the shop or in rented rooms. They were subjected to the discipline of the employer for practically twenty four hours a day and six days a week. Often accommodation was crowded and food poor. Assistants were expected to behave with respect to their employers, to dress well, the women usually wearing special outfits. Shop assistants worked for long hours, often as high as eighty-five a week: there was no half-holiday, and there was no uniform closing time.[63]

Thus shop assistants and domestic servants had many things in common. If dismissed, and shop assistants could be dismissed instantly, both found themselves without a home. Marriage, if not actively discouraged, was difficult and the marriage rate for both was low.[64] Servants probably had better food than most live-in shop assistants. While some servants had to pay for breakages, they were not subjected, like shop assistants, to a fine system for the infringement of numerous petty rules.[65] Wages of shop assistants varied greatly also, but women assistants earned from £10 to £25 a year with board and lodging.[66] Even though conditions in the two occupations might seem fairly evenly balanced there was no doubt that shop assistants were seen as having the more desirable job.

The young girl who is about to start in life has probably a friend in some large shop in Dublin or elsewhere. This friend comes home for a few days' holiday, speaks of the delights of the town, wears her smart clothes, a trailing skirt, and a hat with many plumes, calls herself a 'young lady', in fact assumes a number of airs and graces which dazzle the simple country girl. But she has not spoken of the many weary hours behind the counter, of the importunity and inconsiderateness of the buyers, of the rush during sale times, of the hurried walk from her distant lodgings in the mornings, of the little money saved: these things she has kept to herself.[67]

These things may have been true, but the lack of status of domestic service was the factor underestimated by contemporary commentators. One of the difficulties Michael O'Lehane found in starting a trade union for drapers' assistants was that the assistants felt socially superior to craft or general workers.[68]

Conditions in factories were much inferior – from the point of view of the environment and the type of work – to those in the average middle-class home. Wages were low, 5/- to 10/- a week,[69] and workers had to pay all living expenses from their wages. Not only was the work monotonous but often the dirtiest and most degrading tasks – which men refused to do – were given to women. Many industries were carried on in old houses, basements, out-houses and tenements without proper light, heat or ventilation. In 1917 the working week was generally fifty-four hours. Many learners lost their jobs when they became entitled to enter the National Health Scheme. Laundry workers had to do heavy exhausting work in hot, damp and steamy conditions and, as late as 1914, were only earning 3/- a week.[70] However, hours of work were controlled and workers had evenings and weekends free, and again factory workers enjoyed a higher status than servants. The report of the Women's Advisory Committee on the Domestic Service Problem in 1919 mentioned that:

Except among the lowest class of domestic workers, wages (with which must be estimated cost of maintenance), have for many years been higher than those of workers in comparable occupations, such as clerks, shop assistants and factory employees and they continue to rise.[71]

Yet despite this, domestic service was not able to withstand the competition posed by other occupations, and with the growth of alternative employment domestic service declined.

— *Four* —

LIFE FOR MASTER AND SERVANT
IN IRISH COUNTRY HOUSES

Ireland was well endowed with country houses – possessing over two thousand. A country house was the seat of a landed family or a family of some standing in the locality. While some were very old – a few dating from before the fifteenth century – the great period of country-house building was the eighteenth and the first half of the nineteenth centuries. After the Union in 1801 the Irish nobility and gentry abandoned their town houses and returned to spend more time in their country estates; Dublin, no longer the seat of the Irish Parliament, had lost its attraction. They chose to spend the money they saved on their Dublin houses rebuilding and improving their country houses or building big houses on estates where none had existed before. After the Famine in 1847 many estates were sold, some of the houses being demolished or allowed to fall into ruins. Those who managed to keep their estates had little money for building. Later the agricultural depression of the 1880s and the agrarian troubles which followed left landowners very badly off: even if they could have afforded to build, they were discouraged by the uncertain political situation which lasted through the Home Rule controversy, the struggle for independence, and the civil war of 1922–3.

One of the most popular styles of Irish country houses was a centre block joined to subordinate wings by straight or curving links. It was used not only for the great mansions but also for medium-sized and small houses. Another very popular eighteenth-century style was the three-storey Georgian block which was almost square in shape. There were of course many other styles from the 'Gothic castles' which were popular after the Union to the simple two-storey 'late Georgian' house. Whatever the style of the country house, one of the main considerations of the architect

60

was the location of the servants' quarters. Country houses in Ireland were smaller and plainer than the country houses of England, reflecting less wealth, conservative tastes and a simpler life style. While there were some great mansions such as Castletown, Powerscourt and Emo, the nobility and gentry had smaller houses than their English counterparts; Carton and Barons Court, seats of two Irish dukes, were small by English ducal standards.[1]

'An island – and like an island, a world' was how Elizabeth Bowen described the country house, with its stables, farm and gardens.[2] Country houses built, for the most part, in lonely isolated places approached by long-winding avenues and surrounded, in the distance, by high walls, were indeed little worlds. A young servant arriving on a darkening winter's day, with the rain dripping from the trees, might have found the first sight of her new home dreary and depressing as the horse-drawn car skirted the gravel sweep in front of the house and deposited her at the back entrance. Because, of course, within the country house there were two distinct smaller worlds – that of the gentry who used the front door and that of the servants who never did.

Life for the gentry was, on the whole, interesting and comfortable. The landowner was kept busy as master of a large household and the administrator of an estate: his wife had her responsibilities in looking after the servants and children and generally overseeing the day-to-day running of the home. Children had lessons in the schoolroom with the resident governess or tutor. The women spent a lot of time receiving or making calls which involved a visit by carriage from one local lady to another. The butler or footman brought the visitor's card on a silver salver to the mistress, who then graciously received her guest in the drawing-room for a quarter of an hour's polite conversation.[3] The family went for walks or rode around the estate or perhaps went for longer drives. A major part of the day was devoted to meals which, at that time, were formal and leisurely occasions even when the family was on its own. There was an early cup of tea in bed, followed by an elaborate breakfast served in the dining-room or breakfast room. A wide choice of food – porridge, fish, rashers, eggs and sausages – were kept hot over methylated spirit-burners on the sideboard. Each member of the family helped himself when he arrived. There was lunch at one, afternoon tea at approximately five and dinner at 7.30 or 8 o'clock. Afternoon tea, served in the drawing-room when the weather was cold or wet and on the lawn when the weather was fine, was a major institution of country-house life. Anne Gregory described afternoon tea in the garden in Coole,

the enormous silver tray with the silver teapot with the acorn on the lid, and the enormous silver hot water jug, and then all the food. Masses of scones and butter and honey and strawberry jam bottled by Grandma, and lots of sponge cakes that Mary made and which never tasted so heavenly in the sun.[4]

Family and guests gathered in the drawing-room half an hour before dinner was served and repaired there when dinner was over. 'Amateur theatricals provided one of the ways in which the winter evenings were disposed of where there was sufficient local talent to draw on.'[5]

There were many social occasions. During the summer, garden parties were very popular as well as croquet and tennis parties. Archery and cricket matches were also held, men working on the estate sometimes making up the eleven required for cricket.[6] In winter time there were the neighbouring hunts and the male members of the family, at least, rode to hounds. Lunch was held in different houses after the meets. There were of course many dinner parties and occasional balls. Dinner parties were grand events with lighted glass lamps on table and sideboard, glittering plate and silver on white linen cloths, the ladies in colourful dresses and the men in formal black and white, and in the background, livery-clad footmen silently proffering delectable food. Conversation flowed naturally, in no way constrained by the presence of servants. Having taken steps to confine servants, when not required, to their own part of the house, the gentry were as oblivious to those ministering to their wants as if indeed they were the mechanical devices which eventually replaced them. One lady, who remembered dining in country houses in the west of Ireland, a number of which were subsequently burned down during 'the troubles', wondered if unguarded and indiscreet talk before servants who were treated as if 'deaf and dumb' was not sometimes to blame.[7]

Children of the family played out-of-doors when the weather was fine and took an interest in the animals and hens on the farm. They went for walks or drives with their nanny or governess, or rode on their ponies around the estate. Anne Gregory described adventures in Coole when she and her sister 'stalked' wild duck at the edge of the lake, built tree-houses in the woods and rode their donkey and pony barebacked on warm summer days.[8] When the weather was cold or wet they played indoors – such games as hide-and-seek, blindman's buff, prisoners base, giant, puss in the corner and hunt the hare.[9] As a special treat they went on picnics, to see a cricket match or to a children's party in a neighbouring big house. They went to church with their parents or governess and attended Sunday school. A diary, faithfully kept by four young Bowens, the eldest of whom was twelve when the writing began, gives a wonderful insight into the daily activities, mostly mundane, of young children on an Irish estate towards the end of the last century.[10] Children had their meals in the day nursery; they spent most of their time with their nurses or governess. Some only saw their parents once or twice a day when either the parents visited the nursery or the children appeared all dressed up and on their best behaviour in the drawing-room.

Girls, who usually received their whole education at home from governesses, and single women and widows living with the family – of whom there were many – might have found life dull and boring. They had no specific tasks to do except arrange the flowers, indulge in ladylike accomplishments such as music, painting or embroidery or perhaps involve themselves in charitable works. Elizabeth Bowen, whose uncles went away to school and then to Trinity College and Sandhurst, wrote that 'the past does certainly seem to belong to men'.[11] Frances Cobbe, who lived at Newbridge House, Donabate, in the nineteenth century, wrote how 'The rest of the year, except during the summer vacation when brothers and cousins mustered again, the place was singularly quiet and my life strangely solitary for a child.'[12]

The gentry visited one another frequently and organized shooting parties and weekend parties on their own estates. Lady Fingall mentioned visiting many famous houses such as Carton, Mount Stewart, Adare and Rockingham. Some of these visits lasted a week and Lady Fingall recalled changing her dress as often as five times in the day, for riding, playing croquet and tennis, for shooting, tea and dinner. 'Our frocks were voluminous and our luggage, of course, absurd.'[13] It is not surprising that ladies' maids always accompanied their mistresses on these occasions. A former lady's maid said that there was not a house in Ireland that she and her mistress had not visited. There might be four or five ladies' maids at a weekend house party and there were special bedrooms in the house for them; they ate in the housekeeper's room with the upper servants. They unpacked for their mistresses and sometimes for their masters, as there were very few valets employed in Ireland.[14] Unpacking for ladies who did not have their own personal maids was done by a housemaid. The head housemaid would come with a silver salver on which the guest put the key of her trunk. The maid then unpacked, laid out evening dress and shoes for dinner and put the nightgown on a chair before the bedroom fire to warm. Some ladies had a very frilly nightgown for 'the back of the chair' while sleeping in something much less grand.[15] Katherine Herbert of Cahirnane described her arrival in a large country house where she opted to unpack her 'own modest possessions' herself: the guest room was prepared with a large coal fire, writing table 'wonderfully equipped with everything one could possibly use, even to sheets of various stamps'. The housekeeper, having offered a glass of wine and some biscuits, withdrew, promising to send the maid with hot water.[16]

Weekend house parties were quiet; guests went to church, took walks and drives and perhaps went riding with their hosts, and of course enjoyed large meals. If the weather was bad, women guests might spend the morning in their bedrooms writing letters, the communal rooms in the house, library, drawing-room, smoking-room and morning room were at the disposal of guests and there they could sit and gossip, read or play cards.

There might be twelve to fourteen guests – men and their wives – at shooting parties which usually lasted for three to four days. As well as entertaining these guests and their personal servants, about forty local men were hired as beaters for the shoot; they had to get their meals in the country house also. A former servant described scrubbing a wheelbarrow, lining it with paper and filling it with sandwiches for the beaters who were entertained in the garden. Lunch for the shooting party might be served in the woods where the ladies would join their menfolk. Trestle tables, seats, table cloths, napkins, cutlery, glass, delft, beer and wine were all transported from the main house. Hot food was carried in hay boxes. A cottier's kitchen was taken over for the occasion and the meal served from there by a couple of servants. In some houses, for example Adare Manor, there was special cutlery, glass and delft for the shoot.[17]

The gentry went to Dublin for the main Irish social events of the year.[18] The Dublin season lasted from after Christmas until St

Patrick's Day. Lady Fingall described the grandeur of a state dinner in Dublin Castle during the vice royalty of Lord Spencer with the footmen wearing powdered wigs and scarlet and gold livery. The 'season' in Dublin aped the London season with its balls, parties, entertainments and hunts. At the centre of this social activity was the Castle where, Lady Fingall said, 'we were almost as magnificent as Buckingham Palace with our toy Court'.[19] Lady Ferguson, wife of Samuel Ferguson, first Deputy Keeper of the Records of Ireland, wrote:

Society in Dublin, agreeable at all times, becomes brilliant during winter and early spring, when the hospitalities of the Viceregal Court attract to the city many of the nobility and country gentlemen and their families ... Receptions, dinners, balls and concerts promote gaiety.[20]

Sir John Ross, the last Lord Chancellor of Ireland, also described social life in Ireland:

There was always plenty of social intercourse and lavish entertaining, Dublin, down to the time of the Great War was famous for its dinners. In private houses as many as eighteen courses would be served and the wine was abundant and excellent in quality. The public banquets were simply portentous and the courses were still more numerous.[21]

He also mentioned the 'boundless hospitality at the Castle' during the season, and the large house parties in the neighbourhood of Punchestown during the races.[22] The Dublin Horse Show was another occasion which brought the gentry to Dublin. A former lady's maid said that 'her lady' stayed in the Standard Hotel, in Harcourt St – which also attracted other members of the gentry such as Lady Gregory – when she came up for the show. The maid stayed with her mother who lived in Dublin but came to the hotel every morning to dress her mistress, tidy up, press blouses etc; she was free for the day but returned in the evening to prepare 'her lady' for dinner in the hotel with friends and after that a visit to a theatre.[23]

Besides visiting one another and going to Dublin and other venues for the Irish social round, the gentry spent a lot of time out of the country.[24] Anita Leslie mentioned that the Leslies went away three times a year and after the union they, 'like the rest of the country gentry, took their social life in London.'[25] Household account books kept by Lady Clonbrock record the frequent visits to London by that family.[26] Lady Charlotte Elizabeth Stopford of

Courtown, Co. Wexford, mentioned numerous visits to Windsor in her diary.[27] Lady Fingall tells us that many owners never saw their country houses at their loveliest time, the spring.[28] They were, of course, in London for 'the season'. This social event was recalled by former servants who described their annual sojourn in the capital and also visits to other parts of England during the summer. The Earl of Dunraven and his family spent the summer months – May to August – in Wales. Half the staff – butler, footman, two housemaids, cook and kitchen-maid – accompanied them in the special train they hired to take them from Adare to Rosslare; they brought an immense amount of luggage including three chests of silver.[29] The King-Harman family spent every March in France, as well as the 'season' in London, where their daughters were presented at court.[30] The amount of time that the gentry appeared to spend away from home was a striking feature of life in country houses in Ireland. David Thompson first saw Woodbrook when he arrived from London with Mrs Kirkwood and her two children to act as tutor. He remarked that the hall was dark and unlived-in, as indeed it was, because the family, with the exception of Major Kirkwood, had been away for six months.[31] Many of the great houses of Ireland must have had this unlived-in air for long periods each year. Every effort was made to ensure that the journeys of the nobility and the gentry were as comfortable and free from stress as possible. When Olive Ardilaun, wife of Sir Arthur Guinness, went from Dublin to London the head coachman travelled three or four days before she did with a pair of horses and a groom. The second coachman drove her to Kingstown, where she was met by the Guinness agent, who escorted herself and her maid to the cabins reserved for them which were adorned with flowers from her own garden. A footman travelled on the same boat so that he could look after her at Holyhead and take her and her maid to the reserved carriage on the train: then, at each stopping place – Chester and Crewe – he came to the window to see that they were alright. When she arrived at Euston, 'there would be dear old Horton and my own carriage to meet me'.[32]

Not all country houses were comfortable, prosperous and well-run; Virginia Woolf wrote of Bowen's Court, and especially of its furnishings, 'It is the usual story of Anglo-Irish dilapidation.' 'Innumerable visitors to Bowen's Court recalled the pleasures and sometimes the discomforts of staying in an Irish big house'.[33] When Catherine Stewart married Henry Herbert in the 1860s there was no indoor sanitation in Cahirnane. She said: 'It was horrible. There wasn't a tap or a closet in the house, and I had to make my way out past all those great wet laurels to huts – eight of them, beginning with a giant-sized one down to one for a dwarf or an infant'.[34] St Anne's, the Guinness home, four miles outside Dublin, was so cold and miserable in winter that Olive Ardilaun had two houses in St Stephen's Green converted into what was called a 'perfect small town house' for use during the winter months.[35] The fortunes of houses changed over the years – when they suffered the neglect of an absentee landlord, or fell into the hands of a profligate son, or, perhaps, were inhabited by a solitary ageing owner. These were some of the misfortunes which beset Somerville's and Ross's *Big House of Inver*.

The glories and the greatness of Inver therewith suffered downfall. Five successive generations of mainly half-bred and wholly profligate Prendervilles rioted out their short lives in the Big House, living with country women, fighting, drinking and gambling.[36]

Frances Cobbe, writing in the nineteenth century, implied that many Irish country houses were badly kept. She spoke of recognizing 'that condition of disorder and slatternliness which I had heard described as characteristic of Irish houses'. The occasion was a visit to what she called a 'show' place in Wicklow when the owner invited her to the basement of her home to see some beautiful old china; to the dismay of the lady of the house, the exquisite dessert set was found piled 'higgledy piggledy' with common ware in a cupboard with grape pips and stalks after a dinner the previous summer still on the plates.[37] In the 1920s and 1930s many houses in Ireland suffered neglect caused by rising costs, dwindling incomes and the increasing difficulty in obtaining servants. Molly Keane's novels depict, in a wonderfully evocative way, life in the decaying Irish country house.

To the young general servant working in isolation in the semi-basement of a Dublin suburban home, a position on the staff of a country house would probably have seemed exciting. The presence of other servants, the division of duties, the organization of time, including leisure time, and the provision of special accommodation such as servants' hall or sitting room, would have seemed a vast improvement on her solitary condition. In addition, servants in country houses enjoyed a certain status which devolved from their masters and which varied according to the importance with which society regarded these masters. At country house parties, visiting ladies' maids were ranked in importance according to the standing of their mistresses above stairs. Servants in big houses were paid more than those working in many private houses. Yet in spite of these advantages, the turnover of servants in Irish country houses was more rapid than in Dublin houses, showing that life there was not as ideal or as desirable as it might appear.

There were great variations in the number of servants employed in the country houses of Ireland, the largest households had about twenty, the smallest as few as six. In 1911 William Randall McDonnell, the seventh Earl of Antrim, employed fourteen servants in Glenarn, and this was average for the larger country house.[38] As the family was adult, the two or three servants usually employed in such houses to look after the children were missing. On the other hand, in the same year, there were six servants in Castle Leslie to look after Sir Shane and his two adult sons.[39] The staffs in Ireland were much smaller than in the great houses in the United Kingdom where fifty indoor staff were frequently employed. Lord Aberdeen, the Lord Lieutenant of Ireland, was the only employer who could match that number. In 1911 he had fifty servants, not all of whom lived in the Viceregal Lodge.[40]

Provision for servants, their work areas and their living accommodation, and where these should be sited, were important factors when planning country houses. The servants hall, kitchen, scullery and other service rooms were sometimes located in the basement. Sleeping quarters for the female servants were then usually on the top floor with a back staircase leading from the kitchen area to these rooms. Men servants slept downstairs and the butler had a bedroom adjoining the pantry or plate room so that he could guard the silver. The kitchen and service areas were often found in a separate wing of the house, as they were in Castletown, Co. Kildare. When Castletown was built in 1722 with a central block linked on either side by colonnaded walls to pavilions it was a complete innovation in Ireland and became the prototype for many other houses. The second wing often contained the stables and the grooms slept in rooms above the stable while the maids had bedrooms in the kitchen wing. The separation of the sexes was of paramount importance, and great care was taken to see that men and women slept in different parts of the house. In Ireland the wings were almost invariably used for the offices and stables rather than additional reception rooms as was often the case in England. Older houses sometimes had pavilions and linking walls added on, as in Florence Court, Co. Fermanagh, Woodstock, Co. Kilkenny, and at the home of the Pakenham Mahon family in Strokestown, Co. Roscommon.[41] The kitchen there had a gallery, also found in other country house kitchens, from which the mistress or housekeeper could survey the activities in the kitchen, and lower baskets of stores to the cook. One of the advantages of having the kitchen separate from the main part of the house was that the cooking smells, which were strong and pungent as most of the meat was roasted on spits at open fires, did not penetrate into the living rooms. The food had, of course, to be carried to a distant dining-room; as this was seen as a normal part of the servants' work, it was probably given scant consideration. Hotplates were provided in serveries near the dining-room to reheat the food before it was served.

Another advantage of having some of the servants' work zones and sleeping quarters in the wings of the house was increased privacy for the family and their guests. The baize door, which separated the front of the house from the servants' domain, was symbolic of this division. Most staff only used the back staircase and back entrance so that they would not encounter the family or their friends. Main rooms were cleaned in the early morning, bedrooms later in the day. Kitchen staff very often never saw the drawing-room, dining-room, other formal rooms or family bedrooms. Employers rarely visited the kitchen or other servant quarters. A former servant in Dunsany Castle, Co. Meath, remembered Lord Dunsany's only appearance in the kitchen, which was almost as momentous as the event he came to announce – the outbreak of war between Germany and Britain on 3 September 1939.[42] In Rockingham, Co. Roscommon, the home of the King-Harman family, the servants lived in what David Thompson described in *Woodbrook* as 'a dungeon specially made for them'. He observed that it was not any worse than the attics and basements occupied by London servants, however, it was literally underground, and it meant that all the usual out-offices were out of sight: servants came and went through a dark tunnel. According to Thompson 'it shows how the landowners wished to keep apart from the people who served them.'[43] At Barons Court, the Duke of Abercorn provided quite comfortable quarters for his servants but he had them specially built so that they were not in view from the main house.[44]

When Humewood, Co. Wicklow, was rebuilt in 1867, the architect, William White, was criticized by other architects for placing the servants' offices in the basement below the living portion of the house, perhaps causing noise and cooking smells. They said they associated basement kitchens with town houses, and felt that when space was available and comparatively cheap kitchens were better on ground level and at a distance from the living quarters. However Mr White staunchly supported the 'convenience for purposes of attendance and housekeeping' of bringing 'the servants' rooms into the centre of access to all living rooms'. The women servants' bedrooms were, unusually, on the main floor of the house and immediately over the kitchen offices. A flight of stairs connected the offices to the serving room and the servants' entrance to the dining room. These stairs were furnished with what was called a 'tram' for bringing up the dinner. Food was served through a rotating hatch from the kitchen to prevent smells and noise spreading to the rest of the house. The kitchen had a lofty open roof and was positioned beyond the living rooms. The footman's room was convenient to the front entrance. The butler's room, with the plate closets, was at a safe distance from the back entrance, while the cellar, which was also the responsibility of the butler, was nearly opposite. The housekeeper's room was near the china room and still-room which was provided with a small hatch for serving tea on the front terrace. The laundry facilities were arranged so that the various activities occurred in their proper sequence of washing, drying, mangling, ironing and folding with the washing taking place furthest from the living quarters. The nursery wing on the ground floor was connected to the principal bedrooms and boudoir on the first floor by a turret staircase. While White could show that the kitchen offices in Humewood were carefully, and perhaps successfully, planned, the main reasons for placing them in the basement were, in White's own words, 'to elevate the "living" part of the house above the cold and damps of the country as well as to give a greater command of the magnificent prospects of the neighbourhood, and also to give a greater importance to the exterior effect.' The irony of using the cold and damp area of the house for other human beings, the servants, was lost on Mr White.

The staff in country houses was divided into three departments: house, hall and dining room, and kitchen. The housekeeper was responsible for cleaning the house, looking after the linen, providing and storing tea, coffee, sugar, groceries, preserves, cakes and biscuits. Working under her were the housemaids, laundrymaids, and, if there was a still-room, the still-room maid. The housekeeper's room was comfortably furnished as a living room, and usually had cupboards for storing china, linen and other provisions; sometimes these were kept in a separate store-room nearby. The housekeeper's room in Castletown House was large and well furnished – with a mahogany sideboard, dining-table and six chairs, a large couch, armchairs and two walnut cabinets, a gilt mirror and pictures adorned the walls.[45] It provided a fitting setting for the upper-servants meals and leisure moments. The butler ruled over the indoor male servants, the footmen, hall boy and odd man. He was in charge of the plate, the drink and the table linen. The butler's pantry, while primarily a work area with storage cupboards, sink and table for cleaning the silver, also served as a sitting-room for the butler. In large houses there might be a separate store for the plate, a scullery to clean it in and a small room in which a footman, or oddman might brush clothes, clean shoes and trim and fill oil lamps. 'The grandeur of a house could be measured by the number of chefs in the kitchen.'[46] In Ireland very few kitchens had even one chef. The kitchen domain was almost invariably run by a professional female cook who was assisted by kitchen-maids, scullery maids and perhaps a dairy maid. The kitchen was flanked by sculleries, pantries, a larder and a dairy, with the cook's room often located near the kitchen so that she was never far from her responsibilities. For efficiency as well as moral reasons the three departments were planned to facilitate the work and to separate the female sections – housekeeping and cooking – from the male areas – hall and dining-room.

In one way, however, privacy, or at least separation, must be more directly attended to in every house which is to contain both men and women servants. In a word, the work rooms of the men ought to form one division, and those of the women another.[47]

The butler's pantry had to be as near as possible to the dining-room and hall, far from the back door, for the safety of the plate, and with easy access to the wine and beer cellars. Servants, male and female, met in the servants' hall which was placed as conveniently as possible for both sexes. The servants' hall had to be near the kitchen also as it was the servants dining-room as well as the sitting-room for the lower staff. Sometimes the upper staff, butler, housekeeper, cook, valet and ladies maids had breakfast and tea in the housekeeper's room, and when they had eaten the main courses at dinner and supper with the lower staff in the servants' hall, retired to the housekeeper's room to have their pudding.

The number of servants employed in each department varied. In 1911 the Hon. Robert Edward Dillon of Clonbrock, who was unmarried, had ten servants: three in the kitchen, cook, kitchen-maid, scullery maid; three in the hall, butler, footman and hall boy; a head housemaid and two assistant housemaids; he also had a valet.[48] The Earl of Antrim's fourteen servants included cook, kitchen-maid, scullerymaid and dairymaid; butler and two foot-men; housekeeper, three housemaids and two laundrymaids; he also employed a lady's maid.[49] Personal servants, valets, ladies maids and children's nurses, were under the direct control of master and mistress.

There was a vast amount of work involved in the running of a country house in the nineteenth and early twentieth centuries. Lady Fingall described the situation at Killeen, Co. Meath:

The house was difficult of course to light and heat in those days, when we had only oil lamps and candles. There were two boys to do the lamps and keep the fires of wood and turf going, and carry enormous cans of hot water for baths. I believe it took nearly a hundred lamps to light the house, and even then there were many dim corners.

She added that it took fourteen candles to light a large bed-room, six on the dressing-table alone. Someone had a special duty of going around to put out all the candles when the family and guests had gone down to dinner.[50] Some country houses had central heating but this was only in the main rooms and corridors. Tullynally Castle was one of the first houses in the British Isles to have central heating installed; the original system was designed by Richard Lovell Edgeworth, father of the novelist Maria Edge-worth.[51] Most houses were entirely heated by open fires. This meant cleaning out and black-leading grates, setting, lighting and tending fires in all the living rooms and in the family and guest bedrooms. Water-closets were installed in some country houses in the nineteenth century. At Tullynally a four-storey tower for water closets was added to the house about 1800; it was run off rain

water, which was not a very efficient system. There was no run-
ning-water supply in the house until 1875.[52] Bowen's Court had
lavatories installed about 1860, but even as late as 1930, had no
bathroom.[53] Even when there were bathrooms and lavatories, they
were few in number and were supplemented by outside earth closets for servants and by commodes and chamber-pots in bedrooms.
Many of the gentry washed and bathed in their bedrooms, and so
the work of carrying hot water upstairs and slops downstairs continued into the twentieth century. Housemaids had daily routine
jobs as well as some special task such as the weekly cleaning of a
room, cleaning brass and copper.

Kitchens were well equipped with ranges, grills, turnspits, hot
plates and hot closets but lacked extractor fans and refrigeration
and, of course, labour-saving devices. At busy times of the day
they were very hot and steamy, though this was offset, to a certain
extent, by the height of the ceiling in many kitchens. Walls might
be adorned with edifying quotations from the Scriptures, 'Give Us
This Day Our Daily Bread' or 'Man Shall Not Live by Bread
Alone', which are still to be seen in the kitchen of Castletown
House. Work in the kitchen continued from about six o'clock in
the morning – when the kitchen-maid descended in the dark
silence of the big house to light the range, boil a kettle and bring a
cup of tea to the cook – until about ten at night when the final
washing-up and cleaning after late dinner and supper was com-
pleted. All food was prepared from the raw state and this included
plucking and drawing poultry and game, cutting and boning joints
of meat, making preserves, cakes and biscuits, drying herbs, grind-
ing and blending spices. The scullery maid washed and prepared
the vegetables which the gardener brought in daily from the
kitchen garden. Most of her time was, however, spent standing in
front of two deep zinc-lined sinks in the flagged scullery washing
up the endless flow of dirty saucepans, coppers and roasting tins
from the kitchen, and the dishes from the dining-room and servants' hall. Plates were drained on wooden racks and later polished and put away. A former scullery maid remembered that one
day the butler found a smeary plate and he made her wash all the
plates again.[54] Scullery maids sometimes helped with the simpler
jobs in the kitchen such as boiling and dressing vegetables and
making gravies. The cook organized the work of the kitchen, did
the culinary processes which required special skill and trained the

kitchen-maids and scullery maids. She usually made out the menus for the day which she discussed with the mistress. The mistress might visit the kitchen for this daily conference. A former kitchen-maid recalled preparing for the mistress every morning by covering the end of the large kitchen table with a white cloth, laying a slate with the menu written on it on the cloth and drawing an armchair with cushion up to the table. The mistress never came; she would ring the bell and one of the maids would bring the slate up to her. Yet the daily ritual of preparing the kitchen for the mistress's visit continued.[55]

The butler and footmen laid the table in the dining-room and served at table. The silver plate, cutlery and glass was washed-up in the butler's pantry and the silver cleaned every day by the footmen. The butler and footmen answered the front door and attended to departing guests. The butler was responsible for the house and seeing that it was properly locked up at night. Male servants did tasks such as bringing in fuel for fires, cleaning shoes, brushing and cleaning clothes, preparing and lighting oil lamps, cleaning knives, looking after the servants' hall and going on errands.

Spring cleaning in country houses was a formidable task which was often undertaken when the family was away from home. Carpets were lifted by male servants, taken out-of-doors, beaten and brushed. Each room was cleaned from ceiling to floor; the floorboards were scrubbed before the carpets or rugs were replaced. Curtains were removed and washed or cleaned; loose chair covers were removed and washed by hand in the bath. Cupboards and wardrobes were cleaned out and their contents put back tidily. Necessary repairs and redecoration were attended to. This cleaning took a number of weeks; one servant said that it went on from mid April until the end of May.[56]

In addition to the numerous and essential tasks that had to be done in the country houses, chores were devised which today seem quite ridiculous. Newspapers were ironed before they were presented to the master; laces were removed from shoes, washed, ironed and replaced. One footman had to scrub small silver coins to make sure they 'were unaffected by any previous handling of tradesmen'.[57] Many tedious and time-consuming jobs had to be done, for example, shoes and riding boots were polished with a deer bone to fill in the scratches, they were then polished with a cloth dipped in methylated spirit and beeswax.

Servants worked hard, but in country houses they had clearly defined tasks to perform and a detailed work schedule to follow which included some free time. The butler and footmen had some time off in the afternoons between serving tea in the drawing-room about 4.30 and preparing for dinner at 8. Most staff had some free time between two and five, though a former kitchen-maid said she might have about half and hour's rest after lunch. Servants spent their leisure hours in the servants' hall or in their bedrooms, in larger houses there was sometimes a sitting-room for the female staff where they could read or sew. At night servants could play cards or there might be a billiard-table for their amuse-ment; however, as work did not end until about ten o'clock, most staff probably went to bed.[58]

Meal times for servants were usually breakfast at 8, a cup of tea at 10, lunch at 12.30, tea at 4.30 and dinner or supper, as it was sometimes called, at 9, when dinner for the family was served.[59] Meals in the servants' hall were quite formal, with the butler sitting at the top of the table and carving and the house-keeper sitting at the end and serving the vegetables. A former ser-vant said that the cook did not allow the kitchen staff to go to the servants' hall for breakfast, she did not want them 'sitting in cere-mony for one hour', they were 'better off getting on with their work'. So they ate that meal with the cook in the kitchen.[60] People were served in order of importance and the highest-ranking ser-vant said grace. Food for servants was generally good and plenti-ful. In Dromoland Castle in 1877 1.75 lb of meat per day, or approximately 9 lbs per person per week, was allowed for every-one, family and staff:[61] this was at a time when the weekly con-sumption of meat in the United Kingdom (including Ireland) was less then 2 lbs.[62] It was an extremely generous allowance.[63] In the earlier part of the nineteenth century tea and sugar were expensive and were rarely provided by employers, servants having to buy them from a special allowance. If they were supplied, they were strictly rationed – mistresses giving servants a weekly amount of tea, sugar and butter, and this practice persisted into the present century.[64] Beer was the beverage supplied and, even at the end of the century, men servants might be given only beer with their meals.[65] Servants were given an allowance of beer in some of the larger Irish houses into the 1920s and 1930s. At Adare Manor beer was served at 11 a.m. and 6 p.m.[66] In 1908 and 1909 the

Clonbrock family paid beer money allowance of 2/- a week to female servants and 2/6 to male servants; this was £5.4.0 to £6.10.0 a year, quite a significant addition to their wages.[67]

Servants usually had a bedroom to themselves or shared it with one other. Rooms were adequately but Spartanly furnished with iron bed, wash stand, dressing-table and wardrobe. The 'rule' for servants' rooms was, according to Robert Kerr: 'all private rooms to be equal to those of a similar class of persons in their own homes – perhaps a little better, but not too much so'.[68] An inventory of servants' bedrooms in Castletown House shows that some of the furnishings were probably cast-off items from the main part of the house. Carpets or rugs were often described as 'worn', or 'much worn', a chair had the cane seat 'broken away', a ewer was 'sound' but the basin 'chipped', a mahogany towel rail was described as 'old'. The drainer of a soap tray was 'chipped and odd'. Of course some of this damage would have been done by servants themselves, but it shows that shabby or broken articles were not replaced.[69]

Not only were bedrooms utilitarian and stark, the whole region occupied by staff with its dark, narrow passages, poky rooms, brown or green walls and linoleum-covered floors, was in sharp contrast to the large bright rooms with deep carpets and luxurious furnishings in the family part of the house. Personal servants were often much better off than the rest of the staff because they were usually given bedrooms close to the family on the comfortable side of the baize door. Nursery servants and governesses were near their young charges, the lady's maid near her mistress and the valet close to his master. These servants were often most unpopular with the rest of the staff. The lady's maid was usually accused of having ideas above her station. A former lady's maid said she did not mix with the other staff that she had nothing to do with them; 'they were "pretty rough" – I was different'.[70] This aloof attitude, as well as their more comfortable accommodation, their closeness to their employers and the fact that they were not under the jurisdiction of other staff would all have contributed to their unpopularity. Upper-staff rooms were quite comfortable, but their living rooms had to be shared with other staff and visiting servants – as Kerr put it: 'sitting rooms of the servants are "only conditionally private" and may be open to partners of the same rank or "visitors" attendants'.[71]

Beyond the baize door there was another social divide – that between upper and lower staff. A hierarchic society spawned lesser hierarchies – which were even more aware of differences and guarded privileges more jealously. The normal difference between upper and lower servants based only on status was exacerbated in Irish country houses by differences in religion and nationality, because upper staff tended to be Protestant and British, while many of the lower staff were Catholic and Irish: 68 per cent of servants were Protestant and 44 per cent were born in Britain. Protestants were favoured for the more responsible positions of steward, butler, housekeeper and cook – 90 per cent of butlers and footmen and 75 per cent of cooks, housemaids, parlourmaids and hall boys were Protestants. Catholic employees only equalled, or almost equalled, Protestant servants in the lower status positions as kitchen, scullery, laundry and dairy maids and grooms. Employers always favoured their co-religionists as personal servants and as the gentry in the 1911 country houses were 93 per cent Protestant and only 7 per cent Catholic, ladies maids, valets and children's nurses were invariably Protestant.[72] Stephen Gwynn, describing the congregation at Sunday service in a church in the west of Ireland, said it included about a score of people from the 'great house five miles off'. The ladies were elaborately gowned and the ladies maids and footmen, who obviously accompanied them, 'were even more exotic'. Other servants, not mentioned, were probably joining the Catholics whom he said were 'streaming over to mass' in the 'little chapel' nearby.[73]

Young servants were trained by and were responsible to upper servants whom they regarded as their real masters, often they were very hard task masters indeed. Ann, the cook in Cahirnane, was described as 'angelic' to the family and 'brutal' to her kitchenmaids 'She worked them hard and would teach them nothing, often locking herself into the larder when preparing anything special.'[74] While the jealous guarding of skills was not unknown, especially by cooks, the training given by upper servants was generally considered good, and servants who were satisfactory could progress from scullery maid to kitchen-maid, or from under housemaid to housemaid, or hall boy to footman. The progress of Irish Catholic servants through the ranks to the positions of upper servants was possibly impeded by their nationality and religion. This may have contributed to the dissatisfaction shown by the relatively rapid turnover of servants in country houses. Also, the companionship and empathy which might have been expected to exist among staff may have been lacking.

Many upper servants did not remain long in their positions either. Examination of 44 enumerators' returns for country houses in the 1901 and 1911 censuses showed that, of the 399 servants employed in 1901, only 28 were still with the same families in 1911.[75] In Dromoland Castle, between 1880 and 1886, there were five butlers, three ladies' maids, five cooks and five under-butlers.[76] The personal account book of Luke Gerald Dillon of Clonbrock showed that of ten servants employed in 1888 only one was still with the family six years later.[77] This rapid turnover of upper servants possibly shows that the British servants found working in an alien country both lonely and uncongenial. Elizabeth Bowen said that her first governess found Bowen's Court 'triste'.[78] Lady Fingall recalled a new governess from Dublin who spent quite a lot of time looking out at the wind-swept bog 'her own face as tearful as the sky'.[79] Again Bowen mentions that 'sometimes for days together a family may not happen to leave its own demesne'. She implied that this seemed a dreary and lonely existence to city people or English people; she did not spare a thought for the servants who spent months at a time in these houses, in even greater isolation.[80]

TABLE 7
Percentage of servants in country houses born in different locations
(number in brackets)

LOCAL (SAME CO.)	ADJOINING COUNTY	REST OF IRELAND	GB	ABROAD	TOTAL
16	9	30	44	1	100
(89)	(51)	(165)	(249)	(8)	(562)

Source: 'Domestic Servants in Dublin'.

The Irish servants may have been lonely also because the majority of them worked a distance from home (Table 7). At the time, even the next county was considered a distance. Given the difficulties of travel and their meagre free time, most servants only went home once a year. Those who lived near home were probably the daughters and sons of estate workers and tenants. Ann, the Cahirnane cook, recruited her unfortunate kitchen-maids from among the daughters of lodge-keepers, gardeners or tenants.[81] Domestic service in the local big house was popularly regarded as the usual destiny of these young people. While some landlords recruited local labour, others preferred servants who were strangers, indeed this was the policy in most country houses. There was no local person employed in 39 per cent of the country houses, a further 35 per cent had only one person from the locality on the staff, even though, in some cases there were ten to fourteen servants employed. The smaller households were, on the whole, more likely to employ local labour. Large houses such as Powerscourt, Castletown House and the seat of the Marquis of Downshire, had no local person on the staff, and there were many other similar examples.[82] A former servant who was born on Lord Dunsany's estate in County Meath, where her father was employed, became a housemaid in the castle in 1933. It was the policy there to employ the children of estate workers and she and her sister and brother worked for Lord Dunsany. That servant then got a job as housekeeper in Major McCalmont's home in Thomastown, Co. Kilkenny. The policy in that household was not to employ local labour, and staff were told not to fraternize with the people of the neighbourhood.[83]

Most servants had to spend their leisure time, half days and free Sundays, on the estate, as they lived too far from home and there was nowhere to go within easy distance of the big house. Servants in Rockingham, Co. Roscommon, in the 1930s used to cycle into Boyle on their free afternoons and were, according to a former butler, quite content and happy.[84] Prior to the advent of the bicycle, the only outings servants had were to the local church on Sundays.

Some servants had the opportunity to go to London and other places once or twice a year with the family, and this was an experience to which even a kitchen-maid or young housemaid might look forward. However, this continual 'toing and froing' might in time pall and may have had an unsettling effect. Many servants were left behind and life was very quiet and lonely for them even if discipline was relaxed and the regular routine eased.

There were exciting times during the year. The gentry invariably spent Christmas in their country houses and servants were involved in the festivities. Most employers gave their servants Christmas presents and many had a special Christmas party or dance for the staff.[85] The diary of Lady Charlotte Elizabeth Stopford for Christmas Day 1905 recounted that there was no servants' dance as several of them were in mourning but that it would be held later.[86] Other events might include a dinner for tenants or the coming-of-age of the heir.[87] Of course the presence of visiting servants for shoots or weekend parties also brought excitement and news from the outside world. When in London servants were sometimes treated to a visit to the theatre, the employer paying for the tickets, programme and a cab to bring them there and home again.[88]

The comparatively rapid turnover of staff was reflected in the age structure and marital status of the servants. There was a higher proportion of young staff in country houses than in the Dublin houses – 48 per cent were aged between fifteen and twenty-four compared with 38 per cent in the Dublin houses. The proportion of single female servants was also very high: 95.5 per cent. Only 13 per cent of men were married, this was very low when it is considered that many men servants held jobs for which older servants were preferred.[89] Staff were clearly not as contented as they should have been in situations offering good food, adequate living quarters, security, companionship and the possibility of travel. Reasons for this were probably the lonely positions of many houses, distance from home, living in a foreign country and, in the case of lower servants, the strict discipline often yielded by upper servants, and lack of empathy between the two. 'The staff were really the bosses' according to one former scullery maid; the mistress discovered her scrubbing a 'huge stone passage' one day and was horrified, she ordered that in future the work should be spread over three days.[90] Generally, lower servants did not meet or speak directly to the gentry, they had to communicate with them through the upper servants; the butler or housekeeper might promise to 'speak to the master or mistress' about some matter. Life for upper servants was easier – there was less drudgery, more interesting work, greater comfort, higher esteem and usually a closer relationship with employers.

Besides personal recommendation, the usual methods for recruiting staff for country houses were registry offices and newspaper advertising. As English staff was favoured by country house owners – many of whom considered that first-class servants were not available in this country[91] – English registries were used; two very famous agencies in Marylebone, London, Massey's and Mrs Hunt's were popular with the Irish gentry.[92] Certain agencies in Dublin, such as Kennedy's in O'Connell St and Morrison's at 20 Upper Merrion St, specialized in providing staff for country houses.[93] The gentry did not generally advertise for servants, but answered servants' advertisements. It was only in 1913 that an advertisement for a butler or footman was noticed in *The Irish Times*, showing the difficulty which was being experienced in obtaining servants at that time. Generally servants did not move from middle-class homes to country houses. The gentry either recruited young people who were trained on the job by upper servants or they sought experienced servants who had been trained in that way.

All servants in country houses wore uniform. Women often had to supply their own, while male servants had their liveries supplied by their employers.[94] The provision of the outfit required for girls in the big house was such an obstacle for some parents that they put their daughter into laundries or daily work or as 'slaveys' in comparatively poor households instead. A kitchen-maid entering service in 1918 had to have cotton dresses, white caps, black stockings and twelve white aprons with bibs. Her mother could not afford the aprons so she got a dozen flour bags, ripped and boiled them and made 'twelve beautiful white aprons'.[95] Women servants wore cotton print dresses, usually in blue, pink or lilac with special caps and aprons showing the rank of the wearer – housemaid, cook, or nurse. Housekeepers wore black silk dresses. The humble scullery maid was dressed in a plain cap and cotton dress and a sacking apron.

Footmen in the nineteenth century wore eighteenth-century dress, a knee-length coat, a long waistcoat and knee breeches often made of plush, silk stockings, and for evening wear, buckled shoes or pumps and a wig.[96] Servants' uniform was often based on styles no longer fashionable, presumably to differentiate between servants and their masters and mistresses. Parlourmaids about the turn of the century wore caps with streamers which had been worn by ladies thirty years previously.[97] The wig remained in fashion well into the century and was replaced by powdered hair. After 1870 footmen wore black suits with brass buttons and waistcoats striped horizontally for indoor servants and vertically for outdoor servants; the footmen's fancy waistcoats might be in the racing colours of his master.[98] George, a footman, in the early years of the present century, wore doeskin breeches, white lawn shirt with lace cravat, long silk stockings, shoes with silver buckles, black velvet waistcoat and maroon tail coat. It took this elegantly attired servant two hours to powder his hair and dress to serve dinner. When travelling with his employers to their estate in Ireland, he sat in the 'dickey seat' of the carriage wearing outdoor livery 'a smart ensemble in dark chocolate brown, with yards of gold braid and buttons, a rolled brim 'topper' with a cockade and smart leather gloves'.[99] The butler wore morning suit, short jacket, until noon, he then changed into a tail coat, stiff shirt, butterfly collar and white tie. In the twentieth century, the chauffeur adopted the riding breeches and gaiters worn by his predecessor, the coachman.

While many of the gentry sought to distance themselves as much as possible from their servants, others were much friendlier and took a kindly interest in them. The Aberdeens made an effort to break down barriers. They founded a club to provide recreational and educational facilities for servants. Staff paid an annual subscription of 1/-, and classes, social meetings and entertainments were organized for them. This and other philanthropic actions led to rumours that servants in the Aberdeens' homes were behaving in most unconventional ways. One such rumour stated that visitors at the Viceregal Lodge in Dublin were liable to be escorted into dinner by the butler or housekeeper, rather than by a members of their own social class. These stories, which persisted over a number of years, were investigated by Queen Victoria and later by King Edward VII, and proved unfounded.[100] The royal curiosity shows the importance attached to the manner in which the household of the sovereign's representative was run. The story also shows that the attempts made by the Aberdeens to take a more personal interest in their servants must have been quite unusual, obviously misunderstood and possibly considered dangerous.

— Five —

A CAREER IN SERVICE

Most servants did not seem to consider service as a career: the fact that so few men – who usually regarded work as a career – were servants could indicate that this was true. To women it was a temporary occupation until they married, this is clear from the age structure of female servants. What is perhaps more interesting is that the age structure of male servants was not very different from that of female servants (see Table 8). In 1881 and 1891 approximately 45 per cent of male servants were aged 15–24, a span of ten years, while 42 per cent were aged 25–65, a span of forty years. Men like women did not remain in service. Some probably left on marriage, either because employers did not want married servants or because there was no accommodation for them; others must have just decided to take up other work. The training male servants got was useful for other employments. The big exodus from service by male servants, however, occurred before they had time or opportunity to attain most of these skills. Thus men must have left service for different occupations altogether.

TABLE 8
Percentages of male and female servants in different age groups

CENSUS	SEX	UNDER 15	15–19	20–24	25–44	45–64	65+
1881	M	9	26	19	28	14	4
	F	6	25	22	27	15	5
1891	M	9	27	19	27	14	4
	F	5	26	21	27	15	6
1901	M	6	23	20	34	13	3
	F	3	24	24	30	14	5
1911	M	3	22	19	37	13	5
	F	2	23	23	34	12	6

Source: Censuses 1881 to 1911. Cen. Ire. 1881, 1891, 1901, 1911.

The fact that domestic service was never properly structured or organized, and that efforts to found trade unions for domestic servants did not succeed, also shows an industry that lacked the force usually exerted by career-conscious workers. The rapidity with which many servants changed their situations, often without good reason, showed workers who were uncommitted and disinterested. There was no recognized training for service, no qualifications, no salary structure, no recognized promotional procedure, and no standardized conditions of work, none of the things associated with most careers. As service lacked these requirements it failed to attract recruits seeking a career, and so the existing situation was perpetuated.

In literature, servants tend to belong to two very different stereotypes, those that were continually moving from one situation to another, and the loyal family retainers. The majority of servants belonged to the first category. Miss Collet's report in 1899 showed that the average length of stay for the majority of servants was just over a year. One servant in five stayed for 6.4 years, and the average for those who stayed over ten was 16 years.[1] Advertisements by servants seeking jobs indicated that they considered two years in one household a long period. It has already been mentioned that the turnover of staff in Irish country houses seemed to have been fairly rapid. Of course some servants remained in the same situation for many years, sometimes for their whole working life. The Clements of Ashfield kept five servants for periods varying from twelve to twenty-three years; there were nine servants with over five years service and thirty-eight with less.[2] Although the turnover of servants in Clonbrock was also fairly rapid, two ladies' maids, Rosella Vincent and Sarah Fuidge, who were first mentioned in the wage book in 1894 were still working there in 1910.[3] They were obviously valued members of the household who received many gifts of money and clothes from the family, not only at Christmas but throughout the year.

Information available on the turnover of staff in two upper-class households showed a relatively high level of stability. Although about half the servants in both households stayed for comparatively short periods, the Dillon family of North Great George's Street had two servants employed for at least ten years and one for at least nine years between 1896 and 1906.[4] Between 1907 and 1921 the Robin Vere O'Brien family had one servant for at least fourteen years, while eight others remained with the family for periods varying from three to eight years. On the other hand, seven servants stayed one year or less.[5] These were probably the type of household in which servants tended to remain – comfortable upper-class homes in which there were a number of servants who were well treated and whose diligence and loyalty were rewarded by increases in wages.

The fact that various awards for loyalty and long service were initiated in a number of countries shows that high turnover was a universal problem. The Society for the Encouragement of Faithful Domestic Servants in America offered cash prizes and bibles to servants of one or more years tenure.[6] It is significant that awards were given for periods as short as one year. In England and Ireland a reward system for long service was started by the GFS. Cards printed in gold were given to servants with seven years service or longer, while gold was not used on the plainer cards presented to those with shorter periods.[7] In 1893 twenty-five cards were presented for periods varying from two to seven years.[8]

The main reason for leaving a situation was, no doubt, because the servant found it unsatisfactory. Some servants had spent short periods in some jobs and moderately long to very long periods in others showing that, if a job was satisfactory, those servants were willing to stay. Some mistresses only employed untrained girls as they could be paid less; when they were trained they had to leave to get a better position.[9] In many cases servants left to get promotion or an increase in wages. Except in the bigger houses, promotional outlets were non-existent or extremely limited, and even in households with large staffs, servants often had to change their jobs in order to improve their status. Many servants got the same wages for years.[10]

Even though jobs were generally plentiful, the whole process of finding a suitable situation could be quite difficult and expensive. Most servants would hardly have embarked on it lightly. Letters from the employing class in *The Lady of the House* in 1896 blamed mistresses for the problem of 'obtaining and retaining good servants'. Mistresses were blamed for recruiting the wrong servants, not training them properly and not treating them with consideration and kindness.[11]

Some servants never stayed long in any situation. They were restless, perhaps looking for variety in what was probably a drab and uneventful life. A servant who changed jobs frequently described herself as 'an adventurous person'.[12] The ability to change jobs was the only real power servants had when work conditions were unfavourable. Servants never achieved the collective power which membership of an effective trade union could have supplied. Attempts to organize them in trade unions in Ireland, England, France or the United States met with very little success. In England, abortive efforts to start a union were made in Dundee and Leamington in 1872. The next attempt occurred in 1891 when the London and Provincial Domestic Servants Union was formed. It failed to attract more then a very small number of the city's servants, 562 at its peak in 1895, and was dissolved in 1898. In 1910 a new union called the Domestic Workers' Union of Great Britain was established in London, and shortly afterwards a similar organization was formed in Glasgow; again the union received very little support and had only a membership of 245 in 1912; it was terminated in 1918.[13] Even though there was great union activity in the USA between 1897 and 1917 no effort was made to unionize servants. Attempts were made before that, in the early 1880s and after 1917, but without much success.[14]

The fact that servants usually worked alone or with one other made unionization very difficult. Other reasons were the close relationship between employers and servants, the constant movement of servants from one situation to another, the unwillingness of upper and lower servants to join the same union, the fact that married women looked on service as only a temporary job, and the fear of servants of losing their places and being deprived of references in they joined a union.[15] A servant would suffer much more from a disapproving, if not antagonistic mistress, than a factory girl experiencing strained labour relationships in her place of work. Leonore Davidoff pointed out that, due to their isolation, it was impossible for wives and servants to build occupational or political ties with others in the same position, therefore aspirations for themselves and their children were seen in personal and individual terms.[16] In an article on the GSF in *Past and Present*, Brian Harrison said of class consciousness among women servants: 'class feeling could grow only slowly in an occupational group so penetrated with internal status divisions, so geographically scattered between a host of work places and so close in its contacts with the employer'.[17] Conditions inimical to the formation of class consciousness were also inimical to the formation and sustenance of a trade union.

Former servants and mistresses had no personal experience of a trade union and said that there were no trade unions for servants.[18] During most of their working lives this was true. Attempts were made, however, to found a trade union for domestic servants. In 1911, when Jim Larkin expelled women from the Irish Transport and General Worker's Union (they were readmitted in 1918), a special union for women, the Irish Women Workers' Union, was founded on 5 September 1911 with James Larkin as president and his sister, Delia, as secretary.[19] It collapsed during the 1916 rising but was resuscitated by Miss Louie Bennett early in 1917.[20] In 1919 a Domestic Workers' Section of the union was started and put in the charge of Mrs Margaret Buckley. This branch organized a social club for workers and a registry office in Denmark House; a few months later an unemployment bureau was opened in conjunction with the registry office.[21] The Domestic Workers' Section did not survive and was discontinued during the curfew of 1919.[22] Before the section was disbanded it had about 800 members in Dublin.[23] In view of the number of servants in British trade unions, this was an extraordinarily large number and it seems strange that it did not make a greater impact. Mr W. O'Brien, secretary of the ITGWU, in his evidence to the Vocational Commission said that domestic servants had never been organized. This was corrected by Miss L. Bennett, Mr O'Brien then went on to say: 'some people are not organizable'. Miss Malony objected that it would be difficult but not impossible.[24] There was, however, only one Irish union specifically for domestic servants and it was short-lived. Apart from providing a registry and social club, it does not appear to have achieved anything, not even awareness of its own existence.

In evidence to the same commission, the Joint Committee on Vocationalism, which consisted of the National Council of Women of Ireland, the Joint Committee of Women's Societies and Social Workers and the Catholic Women's Federation of Secondary School Unions, proposed that a home-makers organization should be formed. When asked if they wanted to include servants, Mrs Dempsey, the secretary of the WFSSU said: 'it seems to be the only logical place in which to include domestic servants'. Servants were, according to her, 'completely unorganised', that in the history of the trade-union movement so far, 'not even in England have they succeeded in organizing servants'. She mentioned the difficulty of laying down regulations for domestic servants and in doing so unwittingly highlighted the opposing interests of mistresses and servants and the impossibility of catering for them in one organization.[25] Miss Maloney said that in 1919–20 there was a Domestic Employers' Association which met to set standards for domestic workers and which 'did achieve a remarkable success'. It was a small organization which only existed for a couple of years.[26]

Servants were not completely untouched by the trade union movement. A number joined The Regular Hotel and Club Workers International Union; this was seen in 1913 when the general secretary tried on their behalf to have the by-laws for registry offices changed. In 1923 domestic servants in County Waterford answered an appeal by the ITGWU to support farm labourers in their struggle with the farmers about wages.[27] An interesting fact is that domestic service did not appear to be free of practices usually associated with membership of trade unions. The Sub-Committee on Organization and Conditions in 1919 stated that it would not be possible to allow the servant greater leisure unless 'she is prepared to accept as part of her conditions of service far greater interchange of duties with her fellow workers than has hitherto normally been the custom'.[28] Advertisements which mentioned specific chores that servants would be expected to do, showed that inflexibility existed. Some servants were intimidated by their mistresses but the reverse must also have occurred.

The failure of servants to unite and form trade unions or pressure groups no doubt contributed to the reluctance of parliament to bring in legislation favourable to servants. The domestic servant had the same status in the eyes of the law as a child, while the employer had extensive rights to protect himself against his servants.[29] To terminate employment, a month's notice was required on either side but an employer could dismiss a servant without notice if 'a good or valid reason existed'. A master had to supply his servant with food and lodging but not with medical attention or medicine. A servant had to obey lawful orders, exercise care in carrying out his duties and 'abstain from doing that which he ought not to do'.[30] Very little was done to reverse the legal imbalance. As a result of a couple of cases of extreme cruelty against servants in England in 1851, public outrage prompted parliament to bring in the Apprentices and Servants Act of 1851 which embodied safeguards for young people under eighteen years of age.[31] The only other legislation was the ineffectual act to control registries in 1907. The bill to make compulsory the giving of character notes, and the bill introduced in 1911 to regulate conditions of service, never became law.[32]

Domestic servants benefited from general legislation – the provision of old age pensions in 1908, sickness benefits in 1911, and the Workmen's Compensation Act of 1906. The National Insurance Act of 1911, which was designed to give workers free medical treatment and cash benefits while ill, met with strong opposition from both employers and servants – though principally from the former – in England and Ireland. A threepenny weekly contribution was required from mistress and maid. Mistresses resented being used as tax collectors. The Women's Freedom League urged that the act should be resisted because women were not consulted and it was passed by an assembly which did not include representatives of women. The *Irish Citizen* published articles from the WFL and letters from the public on the subject. The WFL refused to give the government information about employees or to pay any insurance contribution[33] – a course also recommended by others.[34] Women wrote furious letters to the papers saying that the act would divide society and implying that their maids were in agreement with them.[35] However, the Act came into operation in July 1912, and the protests gradually faded away.[36] Some employers paid the whole cost of the stamp and indeed it could form part of the contract between mistress and maid.[37] Employers also opposed the Workman's Compensation Act, 1906, which made them liable for accidents incurred by servants whilst engaged in their employers' business. A writer to the *Lady of the House* said: here in Ireland, where so many people of limited incomes contrive to keep servants, the responsibility fixed upon them by the new Act is distinctly serious'.[38] As employers who did not insure their servants would have to bear the full risk themselves, most decided to accept insurance.[39] The Old Age Pensions Act of 1908, which gave those over seventy years of age, whose income from other sources did not exceed £21 per annum, five shillings a week pension, was a great boon to domestic servants and indeed to thousands of old people.

Those who regard their occupation as a career expect that it will support them during their working life and provide, or allow them to provide, for their old age. Most workers in the nineteenth and early twentieth centuries did not get a pension when they retired. They could expect, however, to remain in employment until they were sixty or seventy, and could save for their old age. Servants, on the other hand, had no security of tenure, found it increasingly difficult to find work after the age of forty, and, if they were unfortunate enough to lose their jobs, also lost their homes.

Many servants were in a position to save. Their daily needs of board and lodging were supplied by their employers, and they had very restricted opportunities for spending their wages. Servants with average or above average wages could put money aside, and many put it in the post office or savings banks. Mr G.T.C. Bartley, author of the old age pension scheme and the manager of the Penny Bank, in evidence to the royal commission on the aged poor in 1895, said that servants were a very much more thrifty class than people thought.[40] However, they were probably only able to provide in a very limited way for their old age. Servants saved for marriage and for periods when they might be ill or out of work and, of course, they helped their families. Some servants possibly saved a lot of money. Mary Davis, a domestic servant who was employed by George Mitchell of 20 Lower Sackville Street, left £941.13.3 when she died in December 1895. Some of this money had been invested in shares in the Royal Bank. Interestingly she bequeathed her money to her employer and members of his family: either she had no near relatives or the Mitchells were closer to her than her family.[41]

As servants got older they found it increasingly difficult to find work. Anita Leslie described how her grandmother did not employ a governess because she considered her too old. When the woman burst into tears and said: 'it's because I'm too old – I'll never get another job', her grandmother, who was sorry for the woman, gave her £5 but did not hire her.[42] In her report in 1899, Miss Collet stated that:

Rough-mannered girls accustomed to service with 'rough mannered employers' found it harder to get work as they got older. As soon as she wanted more than a very small wage she was dismissed and replaced by another young girl. Her background and experience were against her when she looked for jobs requiring a more mature person in a well-ordered house.[43]

THE TRIAL OF MARY ANNE.

MARY ANNE—"I ain't a-goin' to Manchester, or any other place. I go down to Sackville Street on a Sunday afternoon, when the regiments are paradin', from five to twelve.   Lor' bless you, there is nothin' like it in the world, bli'me if there is ! "

His Eminence Cardinal Logue, three Archbishops, and twenty-four Bishops, at the Annual October Meeting held in St. Patrick's College, Maynooth, unanimously adopted the following resolution :—

"Resolved—That from information they have received, the Archbishops and Bishops of Ireland deem it their duty to warn Irish girls against allowing themselves to be induced by certain plausible advertisements, which appear from time to time in Irish newspapers, to go to Manchester or other large towns in England, in the hope of obtaining situations, under favourable terms, in English houses.

"We are assured that unprotected girls are exposed to the greatest dangers in many of those places, and, not infrequently, have been utterly ruined. They never should accept such situations, nor answer such advertisements, without consulting the local clergy, from whom they will obtain the necessary information and guidance."

With the most profound respect and reverence for their Lordships' resolution, "The Lepracaun" is of opinion that there is as much danger to Irish servant girls in parading Sackville Street on Sunday nights as in any English city.

The Lepracaun, demonstrating dangers for Irish servant girls.

THE APOTHEOSIS OF MARY ANN.

MARY ANN: "I don't want any of yer sudden compliments at all.   Just call me what ye did before—a maid-of-all-work, an' if I'm sick let me get Mr. George's benefit and not be behouldin' to you for it."

[As a result of the Insurance Bill a number of mistresses propose to call their servants "companions" and "guests," in order to avoid coming under its provisions.]

A MISUNDERSTANDING.—*His Master.* "Did you take those boots of mine to be soled, Larry?" *Irish Valet.* "I did, sor, and see the thrifle the blag'yard gave me for'm!—'said they were purty nigh wore through!!"

Servants were often the butt of jokes in publications intended for a middle- and upper-class readership. Irish servants, in particular, were lampooned in this way, as these period *Punch* cartoons demonstrate.

Irish Maid. "Do you want a good beating, Master Jimmy, or do you not? Because, if you don't behave yourself this minute—*you'll get both!*"

Mistress. "Poor darling little Topsy! I'm afraid she will never recover. Do you know, Bridget, I think the kindest thing would be to have her shot, and put her out of her misery!"
Bridget. "'Deed, mam, I wouldn't do that. Sure she *might* get better after all, an' then ye'd be sorry ye'd had her kill'd!"

WHEN YOU *ARE* ABOUT IT.—*Magister Familias (parting with his butler).* "Here is the letter, Flanagan. I can conscientiously say you are honest and attentive, but I should have to stretch a point if I were to say you are sober." *Mr. Flanagan.* "Thank you, sor. But when you *are* afther strritchin' a point, sor, wouldn't you, plase, sthritch it a little further, and say I'm *aften* sober!!"

A LITERAL FACT.—*The Young Master (to new valet from the Emerald Isle).* "I say, confound you, what have you been doing with my boots here?" (*The night had been rainy.*) *Pat.* "Shure, sorr, you tould me lasst evening to putt 'm on the thrays!"

Nursemaid (above) in cap and apron. Parlourmaid (above right) with afternoon black dress, starched apron and white streamers to her cap (detail from 'Five O'Clock Tea' by William Powell Frith, 1894).

Kitchen-maid (below) in décolleté dress with lace trim and apron adapted to a bustle, 1890. Parlourmaid (below right) in elegant attire answering a door, 1894. (See P. Cunnington, *Costume of Household Servants* [1974])

A general servant in the 1930s whose duties patently included feeding the hens and minding the child!

A middle-class family at the turn of the century, photographed with their servant — not a common practice.

The assembled staff (above left) at Bessborough, Co. Kilkenny, in September 1908. (Poole Collection, National Library of Ireland)

Female servants (above) at Clonbrock, Co. Galway. The photograph shows subtle differences in dress reflecting the position and contact each had with the 'upstairs world': the girl with the cap, back row left, was the parlourmaid who served tea and showed visitors to their rooms. The woman to the right, with elaborate *broderie anglaise* collar and fancy apron, was probably the lady's maid. The young girl, second row left, was the scullery-maid. The housekeeper, with the heavily beaded silk top, is centre-stage. The priest was in all likelihood chaplain to the household staff.

The terrace garden at Clonbrock (left) in 1901, with afternoon tea being served to the Hons Mabel Crofton, Mrs Dealtry, Ethel Dillon, Katie Dillon, Robin Dillon, Georgy Dillon, and to Lord and Lady Clonbrock.

Badge (right) of the Irish Women Workers Union.

"VORTEX" SUCTION CLEANER

"Now you've this, m'am, I'll stay."

" Vowel " Washing-Machine

The new labour-saving, and labour-replacing, equipment invariably shown being used by a servant. The Siemen's suction cleaner dates from 1911; the prototype washing-machine is from an earlier period, as is the wringer mangle and the Sun knife-cleaner (below) of 1885.

AVOID EXPENSIVE REPAIRS!!!!

"use the A PERFECT MANGLE.

Safety Framing of Wrought Iron.
Breakdowns Impossible.

Wringer & Mangle Pressure Instantly. Applied or Released

Illustrated Catalogue Post Free.

Children Cannot Crush their fingers.
Our name and the word Safety are cast on every machine
ENTWISLE & KENYON Accrington.

SUN KNIFE CLEANER

In *Esther Waters* George Moore described a conversation between Esther and an ageing servant about wages while they waited
to be interviewed for a job. The older servant said: 'Sixteen! I used
to get that once; I'd be glad to get twelve now. You can't think of
sixteen once you've turned forty, and I've lost my teeth, and that
means a couple of pounds off.' She did not get the position, even
at twelve pounds and as she left she said to Esther, 'I'm too old for
anything but charing.'[44] In spite of their experience, older men and
women found less demand for their services.[45]

Certain categories of servants had perhaps a shorter working
life than others. Children's maids or nurses often found themselves
without work when their charges got older or went away to
boarding school. If the nurses were middle-aged they found it difficult to get another job. Sometimes the problem was solved by the
same employer retaining them in another capacity, as a housekeeper, housemaid or perhaps as a daughter's lady's maid. Most
mistresses, however, preferred their maids to be young, so unemployment was a serious problem for middle-aged ladies' maids.
Some, a lucky few, became housekeepers, but this was not a popular type of promotion in the servants' hall, and most mistresses
were wary of upsetting the domestic staff. Also, when it came to
marriage, the lady's maid had two handicaps, 'She had almost certainly ideas above her station and she did not know how to
cook.'[46]

Servants could find themselves out of work and unable to get
another situation from the age of forty-five upwards. It was difficult for them to save sufficient for their old age, especially if that
phase of their lives commenced rather early. Many servants without work, without money, and without a home had to resort to
the county home or workhouse.[47] Census returns from 1881 to
1911 show that a quarter to a fifth of the people in workhouses,
the largest occupational group listed, were servants.[48] (In 1881 servants formed 5 per cent of the total population and this proportion decreased in subsequent years.) As many of the inmates had
not given any occupation, it is likely that a number of these had
been servants also. Domestic servants were the second largest
occupational group in lunatic asylums, about 8 to 9 per cent of the
total, and again there were probably more servants in asylums
whose occupation was not recorded. A comparatively small
number of all inmates were specified as 'hereditarily affected'.[49] It

is safe to assume that many were consigned to asylums because they were old and had nobody to look after them.

There were a number of homes, usually run by a committee of ladies, for elderly Protestant women; some were specifically for domestic servants, others were simply for widows and aged single women, many of whom may have been servants. The Asylum for Aged and Infirm Female Servants, 15–17 Drumcondra Road Lower, was typical of this type of home. It was intended for Protestant servants of good character who from age or infirmity could no longer work: the servants were provided with lodging and coals. It was not easy to get in, the servant had to be recommended by someone who was willing to subscribe £1 a year and at least 4/- weekly for her support. Servants entering the home had to have an iron bedstead, bedding and other articles of furniture. If the subscription was not paid for two weeks, the servants had to leave. Women entering these homes were not destitute, they had to have an employer or friend willing to pay approximately £11 annually, a considerable sum at that time, for their support. The number of people catered for in many of these homes was quite small; there were only twelve inmates in the Asylum for Aged and Infirm Females in 1899. The fate of those women if, for any reason, their sponsorship was discontinued – a not unlikely event if they outlived their former employers – must have been very hard indeed. Some religious orders provided homes for Catholic servants; St Joseph's Asylum, Portland Row, Summerhill was one of these. It catered for about a hundred aged and virtuous unmarried women, many of whom were probably servants, and it was free.[50] When the total number of servants is considered, the percentage that these homes could cope with was small. Katherine Everett née Herbert described visiting a home for old governesses with Lady Ardilaun, 'where on opening the front door we were met, by a smell of cabbage, mutton, and linoleum'. Here, in rooms surrounded by 'a gallery of photographs of late pupils', elderly women whiled away their last days.[51]

Some servants were provided for by their employers until they died; they either continued working, no doubt less actively, or were regarded as retired.[52] Mervyn Wall in Hermitage describes how Tony, the hero, visited his cousin's farm as a schoolboy and loved to accompany old Martha, the retired housekeeper, whose only duty now was to feed the hens.[53] Retired servants were sometimes given cottages on the estates or allowed to go on living in them until they died. In 1911 the Earl of Antrim had a retired butler, and the Earl of Portarlington had a retired housemaid, living on their estates.[54] Frances Cobbe writes of how her 'good nurse was settled for the rest of her days in a pretty ivy-covered cottage with large garden, she had an old woman as servant who had been under-dairymaid to my great great grandfather'.[55] Elizabeth Smith described giving food and firing to ten pensioners, all people who had worked for them, some no longer living on the estate.[56] Lord Aberdeen, when he grew up, gave his nurse a modest pension.[57] The O'Brien family of Cahirmoyle gave generous pensions to some of their servants in 1903,[58] and between 1906 and 1912 six retired servants on the Powerscourt Estate got a weekly pension of about 5/-; they also seemed to have cottages on the estate.[59] Servants who worked for the gentry for a number of years had better prospects of an independent old age than those who worked in smaller households. Of course, even on an estate, only a small number could be provided for in this way.

A loyal servant who worked many years for the same employer might have expected to be remembered in her master's will. However, only about 20 per cent of employers left bequests to servants and most of these were for small sums of money – £3 to £10 – or, at best, the equivalent of one year's money wages.[60] It must be remembered that this would provide for a servant for a much shorter period if she had to pay for accommodation while she looked for a new situation or considered how she would spend her old age. Very few servants got sufficient money from their masters to live on in their old age. In 154 wills probated in Ireland between 1891 and 1922 only six servants got sufficient money to allow them to do that – these included annuities of £25, £26 and £50. Two servants got three-quarters and one quarter of the residue of an estate – value unknown. Only one servant received what was undoubtedly a valuable bequest – £1500, furniture and and a house in Waterloo Road.[61] It is impossible to know exactly how many servants benefitted under the wills examined as some employers did not name servants but left sums to those who, for example, served them for five years or more.[62] Employers usually stipulated that the servant had to be in their employment at the time of their death to benefit, usually adding, 'and not under notice to leave'.[63] There were great variations; some servants got generous bequests after comparatively short service, others with long service and, at an age when work was difficult to obtain, got little or nothing.[64] Where an employer expected his widow or other members of the family to maintain the household after his death he usually did not leave bequests to servants, he probably did not feel any onus on him to provide for them. Also, many elderly employers had only young servants who were, no doubt, in their employment for short periods. Looking after servants in this way was in the paternalistic tradition which gave employers responsibility for their servants even when the latter had grown too old to work. Very few employers in Ireland sought to fulfil this type of obligation when making their wills. Certainly servants could not count on the generosity of employers to provide for them in their old age.

Employers had an abiding fear of hiring a dishonest or immoral servant, hence their insistence on receiving good references from former masters. While this is quite understandable as the servants were being accepted into their homes, it should not be taken as an indication that domestic servants were more likely to have criminal tendencies than other workers. In Ireland indoor servants were approximately 10 per cent of the working population between 1881 and 1901 and they accounted for less than 3 per cent of convicted criminals.[65] In 1898 46 per cent of convicted prisoners were labourers as against four per cent servants.[66] Criminal records of 983 convicts included only eight servants, less than 1 per cent of the whole.[67] Five of these servants were convicted of theft, one of abduction, one of concealed birth and one of manslaughter.[68] An interesting fact is that, while most servants were women, four of these were men. Male servants were much more likely to be involved in criminal activities. While they accounted for about 7 per cent of all indoor servants, the percentage of male servants in prison varied from 20 to 40.[69] Two of the larcenies were committed by women who had left or been discharged and had returned to rob their former employers. One, a forty-eight year old woman, Mary Sherlock, said that the conduct of her employer towards her was 'very bad' and she threatened to bring an action against him. He promised her money if she refrained, but as he had not paid after two years she returned and stole £15. She was sentenced to twelve months' imprisonment for housebreaking and robbery. The man sentenced for abduction had first of all seduced a fifteen-year-old fellow servant, when discovered and charged he had absconded with the girl. The maid accused of a concealed birth had killed her new-born baby, her second illegitimate child. With the exception of manslaughter, these crimes are representative of those usually associated with servants – theft and sexual offences. The majority of convicted servants were, no doubt, guilty of theft; many of those guilty of prostitution would have been recorded under that 'occupation', or would have ended up in workhouses not in jails.[70] It was also found in England and France that servants were less likely than other occupational groups to be involved in criminal activities.[71]

Servants were easily caught and accused, and if larcenies occurred they were usually the first to come under suspicion; it was easier for employers to attribute wrong-doing to servants than to members of their own family. It was easy to allow the crimes undoubtedly committed by some servants to grow into a general distrust of all servants; also, distinctions were not always made between relatively minor offences and serious crimes. Many servants were involved in petty larceny of food and drink. Elizabeth Smith complained about a servant who was 'lazy, stupid and dishonest', she stole eatables and wearables.[72] Very few former mistresses mentioned dishonest servants. One recalled a girl who was about to get married and set up home, she helped herself to 'bits and pieces' such as cups, cutlery and saucepans. This kind of dishonesty was not unusual according to the mistress.[73] Many thefts by servants would never have been discovered and, if they were, most employers did not bring their servants to court, they merely discharged them. It was one of the most common reasons for sacking servants.[74] Some employers even kept what they considered 'good servants' knowing that they were 'light fingered'; they were just more careful about locking up valuables. One mistress simply went to the maid's room regularly and 'recovered' her belongings.[75]

The majority of servants in Ireland would appear to have been honest. Most of those who were not were probably engaged in petty larceny. Some excuse could be found for their behaviour: 'No people contemplate so strikingly the unequal distribution of wealth: they fold up dresses whose price contains double the amount of their year's wages; they pour out at dinner wine whose cost could have kept a poor family for weeks.'[76] On the other hand, most servants were not in need as were other sections of the population at the time. If they valued their positions, they were not likely to jeopardize them by stealing from their employers. Two of the five cases of larceny mentioned were committed by servants after they had left their employment. A danger which employers feared was that a servant would give inside information to thieves outside the household. In the case of serious crime this was a more likely danger.[77]

The most prevalent problems concerning servants, apart possibly from petty theft, were those involving illicit sexual relations. In nineteenth-century France 'the domestic servant class was clearly the greatest supplier of prostitutes, in addition to having the most illegitimate births'. An investigation into prostitution in the early twentieth century in London found that 293 out of 830 prostitutes, 35 per cent, had been domestic servants.[78] The mothers of illegitimate children were frequently domestic servants. Servants were particularly vulnerable to sexual exploitation by the master, sons and visitors to the house in which they worked. They were often regarded by the employing class as inferiors who could be abused with impunity. If the servant complained to her mistress she not only lost her job but was probably blamed for the indiscretions that had occurred. Unlike other workers, servants had virtually no private life. They were often lonely, deprived of the companionship of members of the opposite sex and so were particularly vulnerable: employers and their friends frequently took advantage of this situation. In large houses servants were sometimes either seduced by male servants or formed liaisons with them. A former lady's maid who visited many of the big houses in Ireland said it was not unusual for women servants to have men in their bedrooms at night.[79]

Most young girls going into service around fourteen years of age would have been innocent of 'the facts of life'. A former servant who started work in 1913 at the age of sixteen said that she did not know 'where babies came from'. She was soon 'educated' by the parlourmaid.[80] Mrs Layton in Life as We Have Known It described going into service in Kentish Town at fifteen where, soon after her arrival, the mother died in childbirth: 'I knew nothing of the facts of life … and I really cannot say how I did get my knowledge.'[81] Norah Ryan, Patrick MacGill's heroine in The Rat Pit, was also innocent: 'no one had ever explained to her why she was and how she had come into being.'[82] Obviously not all servants were innocent victims of sexual liaisons. Some may have had dreams of marrying a son of the house or a friend of the family and in this way escaping from service.

In Ireland where the majority of the population were strict Catholics, very much under the influence of the Church, there was a puritanical attitude to sex and very little tolerance for pre-marital sex or prostitution. A pregnant servant could expect little sympathy from her mistress, or indeed from her parents, many of whom were probably kept in ignorance of their daughter's condition.

The mother of an illegitimate child was almost always treated as a pariah. Dr Kirwan, parish priest of Kilcummin [Co. Galway], expressed views which were typical of those held throughout the country: 'I do not think there are six men in the parish who would marry women who had illegitimate children by other fathers; ... and the woman who has lost her virtue, unless repaired by a subsequent marriage, loses with it for life her character and her caste.'[83]

When girls seduced by masters, members of his family or others became pregnant, they were often dismissed instantly without a character and literally put out on the street. Some returned home, if their families would take them in, many had to go to the workhouse. In spite of the dire consequences for the women, seduction of servants and premarital sexual relationships seem to have been fairly common among servants in Ireland. The mothers of illegitimate children were frequently domestic servants.[84] Many servants and employers had experience of working with or employing servants who had illegitimate children.[85] Some servants had experience of masters who made sexual overtures to them or to other servants.[86] One servant who was interviewed by the mistress for a job was told that, while she was satisfied, the master would have to approve before she could be engaged. A week after she started work the master came to her bedroom at night; she threatened to tell his wife and when he left the room she stole quietly out of the house – it was now after midnight – and walked to the home of a previous employer who took her in.[87] Another servant said that the housemaid where she worked was known as the cook's sister, but was in fact her illegitimate daughter. The child had been in The House of Mercy, Baggot Street, when she left there she got a job where her mother was working.[88] Incidents such as these show that many employers were compassionate and willing to engage servants who had illegitimate children and indeed to engage the child also. Girls who worked as farm servants in Ireland seemed especially vulnerable to seduction by the farmer, his sons or farm workers. A story is told of farm lads who, annoyed that they were not hired, shouted after a farmer who had engaged a servant girl instead: 'I suppose you paid £9 for her, and she'll have a child with you for the Christmas.'[89] Some farmers took precautions to avoid, as far as possible, illicit liaisons between farm servants. In *The Farm by Lough Gur*, Mary Carbery tells the true story of a family who lived on a farm in Co. Limerick. The maids slept upstairs while the farm boys had a room in the yard, 'except for meals and prayers they were not allowed inside the house, nor was any sort of friendship allowed between them and the maids'.[90]

Prostitution was commonly regarded as the likely fate of domestic servants who were unfortunate enough to lose their situation through illness, or as a result of illicit sex or for some other grave reason. An early report of the GFS in Dublin about girls who went into service said: 'from time to time there comes news of those that are gone, sometimes glad tidings, but alas, too often tales of shame and misery, of wasted lives spent in the service of sin or vanity instead of in the service of God'.[91] Certainly illicit sexual relations led to the loss of situation, resort to the workhouse and possibly prostitution. Crimes such as concealment of birth, infanticide and suicide often followed. Such a case was reported in *The Irish Times* in 1883, when a farm servant was found hanging from the rafters in a cowshed. It appeared she was seduced by the farmer's son. When it became obvious that she was pregnant, her mistress showed no mercy, the girl was told on Friday that she must leave on the following Sunday; that night she killed herself.[92] In France, servants accounted for a disproportionate percentage of those who committed suicide.[93]

In an effort to save girls who had a first illegitimate baby from a life of sin and degradation, the Report of the Viceregal Commission on Poor Law Reform in Ireland in 1906 recommended that these girls should be sent to a special institution kept by religious or philanthropic persons. It was hoped in this way that girls who had one 'misfortune' would be removed from the company of habitual offenders. The report described an experiment in the Limerick workhouse where those with first illegitimate babies were kept in a special ward under the care of a sister of mercy.

Most of these girls were placed in service. This was a very good development as it gave girls who were perhaps innocent victims an opportunity to lead a normal life again.[94]

Servants were occasionally involved in more serious crimes such as manslaughter and murder. A couple of notorious cases occurred in England. Lord William Russell, an uncle of the Prime Minister Lord John Russell, was murdered by his valet. Two women, who were under notice to leave their situations, murdered their mistresses. In two of these cases theft and resentment against difficult employers were the causes of the crimes. In the third case, a particularly gruesome and horrific one, the servant was drunk at the time of the murder.[95]

A murder occurred in Ireland in 1880 which received a lot of publicity in the national newspapers. A servant, Margaret Skeen, murdered, not her employer, which was more usual, but her successor. Margaret was engaged by a Mr Brabazon, who lived with his sister and her daughter near Drogheda. She was happy there for some time, but then the two ladies left and she was alone in the house with her employer. Margaret said that she discovered then that he drank to excess and 'an improper intimacy arose which resulted in her master brutally ill-treating her on several occasions'. Finally she left and went to live nearby with her sister who was married to Mr Brabazon's other servant. She asked Mr Brabazon for her 'discharge' which he refused to give, consequently she could not get another situation. Margaret said that she became desperate and started to drink. Meanwhile Mr Brabazon hired another servant.[96]

On 7 January 1880 Mr Brabazon and his outdoor servant, Margaret's brother-in-law, went to Drogheda leaving Emma Bouchier, who had replaced Margaret Skeen, alone in the house. When they returned at 11 p.m. they got no answer and had to get into the house through a window. They found Margaret with blood on her face and arms, and then discovered Emma's body in a well in the scullery with wounds on the head, neck and chest. Margaret Skeen had then rifled Emma's belongings and stolen some articles of clothing and some trinkets.[97] The judge who tried the case felt that this 'if possible aggravated the crime'. It was stated afterwards that there was no suggestion that an improper relationship existed between the unfortunate girl who was murdered and her employer.[98] Margaret Skeen was found guilty of manslaughter and sentenced to penal servitude for life on 2 March 1880. Her own explanation of the event is contained in her unsuccessful petition to the lord lieutenant: 'while labouring under the effects of drink and blinded by jealousy, I committed the crime'.[99]

These cases, which were followed with great interest by both employers and servants, had the effect of making the former even more particular about the credentials of prospective employees.

Six

DECLINE IN DOMESTIC SERVICE

Problems which beset domestic service such as the need for formal training, control of registry offices, standardization of conditions and work practices, and unionization of workers, were never solved, they just faded away with the virtual demise of service. The decline started in the 1880s and although gradual at first, concern about it appeared in magazine articles and GFS reports in the 1890s.[1] The report of the GFS for 1901 stated that: 'the lack of servants and the demand for them is greater this year than last'.[2] A decrease in the number of members in service and in the number of good service premiums was noted in 1902.[3] Between 1890 and 1906 the number of applications for servants to the GFS more than doubled, showing the growing difficulty in obtaining servants, while the number of girls placed in 1906, 112, was about the same as in 1892 and 1886.[4] In *The Lady of the House* in 1896 a mistress complained that

wherever one goes, one hears so much of the – almost – impossibility of finding good servants, and, if found, keeping them, that it has become evident that there is a serious hitch somewhere in the fitting-in of this department of domestic affairs with the requirements of modern life.

Readers were asked to submit their views on the causes of the difficulty.[5] One of the many responses in the following month mentioned the growing independence of the 'lower classes', and said that 'a good servant is becoming the rarest thing on earth'.[6] An article in *The Irish Homestead* in 1903 deplored the dearth of 'respectable' servants which was becoming greater each year and described it as a 'national canker'.[7] What was described as 'an extraordinary prejudice' existed in Ireland against domestic service.

Many an intelligent farmer's daughter considers it a great come down in the world, a disgrace even, to become a servant. A sense of slavery and servitude seems to have attached itself to the idea of domestic service ... The mode of life, the treatment received, the opinion in which he or she is held, removes the servant an infinite distance from the slave. The name 'servant' is regarded with prejudice when it is connected with domestic duties, but no such objection attaches to it when it refers to work done on a railway or for the State.[8]

The census returns showed that there was a drop in the number of servants in each census year from 1881 to 1926. While the population of England and most Western countries was rising, that of Ireland was falling. The decrease in population meant that the proportion of servants to the whole population did not change as rapidly as the drop in numbers might suggest, it did go, however, from five per cent in 1881 to three per cent in 1911 (see Table 9). Between 1881 and 1911 indoor female servants in England and Wales did not decline in number but increased at a much slower rate, which did not keep pace at all with the growing population.[9]

TABLE 9

Number of indoor servants, male and female, in Ireland, in census years 1881–1911, showing servants as a percentage of the working and total populations

CENSUS YEAR	NUMBER OF SERVANTS	% OF WORKING POPULATION	% OF TOTAL POPULATION
1881	250,381	10.5	5.0
1891	211,095	10.0	4.5
1901	175,500	9.0	4.0
1911	135,325	7.5	3.0

Source: Census of Ireland, 1881–1911

There was no obvious reasons in Ireland such as there were in England – industrial growth and the 1914–18 war, when it was reckoned that 400,000 women left service for factory work and many never returned[10] – for the decrease in the number of servants. Those who left were popularly regarded as emigrating or going into shops, factories or offices.[11] There is no doubt that many emigrated. The number of emigrants rose from an annual average of 50,172 in 1871–81 to 59,733 in 1881–91.[12] Emigration affected young girls, especially those from lower class rural families, more than any other group, the class from which most Irish servants were recruited.[13] The number of females emigrating in 1881–91 rose by 92,100 on the previous ten-year period. It dropped after that, but still 230,868 and 173,284 females emigrated in 1891–1901, and between 1901–11 respectively.[14] About 80 per cent of these were at an age when they could have worked as domestic servants. The result was that while there were 233 female indoor servants to every 1000 families in 1881, this had fallen to 140 per 1000 in 1911.[15]

The vast majority of Irish emigrants at the time went to the USA[16] and most of these entered domestic service.[17] Robert Kennedy, in *The Irish*, noted that there was a large increase in the number of Irish immigrants who gave their occupation as 'servant' in selected years between 1875 and 1911. In 1875 about five thousand servants left Ireland to work in the US; the number increased by nearly three thousand in 1881 and by a similar figure in 1891; in 1901 the increase was less important and it dropped to 178 in 1911.[18] Of course many of those who had no specific occupation, which would have included most of the women, also became domestic servants.

The stereotype of the American servant was the immigrant and of all immigrant groups, the Irish symbolized the typical American servant:

Even in the South, where traditions of Negro servitude held sway, the Irish were recognized as the typical white servant. The Irish seemed to be everywhere and to have 'solved an immense difficulty' by supplying a substantial number of servants. Several circumstances account for this impression. The Irish, first of all, were the largest unskilled immigrant group in the nation and, until the twentieth century, provided two to three times more servants than any other foreign nationality. Additionally, Irish servants worked in every section of the country ... Popular writers created an image that solidified this identification. American newspapers and magazines featured the colorful Hibernians, characterized as Paddy and Bridget, as stock subjects in jokes, cartoons, and anecdotes about servants. The impact of this impression was powerful and lasting.[19]

A high percentage of Irish women who emigrated to Australia became servants. There, also, the Irish servant was seen as typical of servants in general. As in England and the US, she became the butt of cruel jokes and cartoons; lampooning the Irish female servant was known as 'Biddyism'. This perception of the preeminence of the Irish servant was due, not only to their number, but to their concentration in particular areas of cities and to the fact that they usually worked as general servants and remained longer in service than other nationalities due to late marriages.[20]

The fact that women who might be considered as fleeing from service in this country became servants in the USA and Australia should not come as a surprise. It was probably the only work available to them and in America, a more democratic country than Ireland, domestic servants probably enjoyed a higher status; also the girls were strangers in a foreign country without preconceived ideas about their own social position within that society. It was also found in England that girls who rejected service in their own country became domestic servants when they emigrated to the colonies.[21]

It is not as easy to discover where girls who remained in the country, and who would have become servants, found alternative employment. The economic development of Ireland lagged behind that of all other north western European countries.[22] Ireland could not offer the factory jobs of thriving industrial countries like England and France, or the new opportunities for women created by the First World War.

TABLE 10
Percentage of females in the different occupational classes in the Irish censuses, 1881–1911

CATEGORY	1881	1891	1901	1911
1 professional	3.4	4.4	5.3	8.2
2 domestic*	39.9	37.3	35.4	34.0
3 commercial	0.2	0.4	0.9	2.3
4 agricultural	15.0	15.4	15.6	13.8
5 industrial	41.5	42.5	42.8	41.7
TOTAL	100	100	100	100
NO. WOMEN OCCUPIED	634,793	592,140	549,874	430,092
% OF FEMALE POPULATION	24.0	24.8	24.0	19.5

Source: Cenus of Ireland, 1881–1911

ADJUSTMENTS MADE IN CENSAL CATEGORIES
1   139,092 females – almost all wives and other near relatives of the heads of families returned as housekeepers – were removed from 'occupied females'; and the 'domestic class' in the 1881 census and put into the 'indefinite and non-productive class' in accordance with a change introduced in the 1891 census.
2   For comparison purposes scholars were removed from the 'professional class' and 'occupied class' and put in the 'indefinite and non-productive class' in the 1881 and 1891 censuses to keep them in line with a change made in the 1901 census.
    * Domestic class includes outdoor servants, hotel and club workers, charwomen, washing and bathing service, hospital and institutional services as well as indoor servants.

The actual number of women in agriculture and industry decreased steadily between 1881 and 1911, but due to the decrease in population their position as a proportion of the occupied female population remained remarkably constant. It was only between 1901 and 1911 that there was a real decrease in employment of women in agriculture. While there were changes within industry between 1881 and 1911, there was virtually no change in the proportion of the total female work force employed in industry. There was a significant increase in the professional class and commercial class between 1881 and 1911. While most of the increase in the former probably came from the middle and upper-classes – daughters who hitherto would have remained at home as dependents – some were, no doubt, women who might in earlier times have become servants, and now became teachers or entered the religious life. Many probably got jobs, as the women's magazines said, in offices or shops. Some of those who abandoned service or who would formerly have sought work in service, obviously stayed at home – like middle-class girls – as there was an appreciable rise in the number of unemployed women in Ireland between 1901 and 1911 (see Table 10 above). Some of the occupations in which the greatest changes occurred between 1881 and 1911 and also those which might have been expected to absorb those who abandoned service are shown in Table 11 (overleaf).

The decline in service was steady and increased over time.[23] In 1911 there were 7970 male indoor servants in the twenty-six counties, this had fallen to 1818 in 1926. In the latter year indoor domestic servants represented only 5 per cent of the population of the twenty-six counties.[24]

The reason for the growth in emigration was possibly due as much to dissatisfaction with life in Ireland, especially rural Ireland, as it was with dissatisfaction with domestic service. This was probably true, especially at the end of the last century. Robert Kennedy gives the subordinate status of women in rural areas in Ireland which he maintains was greater than in other European countries as a reason for women leaving Ireland.[25] From Famine times there was a tradition of emigration to the United States especially in country areas. The attractions of life there and in England were well known from those who had emigrated over the years. A knowledge of the English language made integration relatively easy. Single people, especially single women, found it easier to emigrate and there was a growing number of single people in the Irish population after the 1870s.[26]

TABLE 11

Number of women in certain occupations in 1881 and 1911, showing each as a percentage of the total occupied female population in that year

OCCUPATIONS	1881		1911	
	NO.	% OF OCCUPIED	NO.	% OF OCCUPIED
nuns	5282	0.8	8887	2.0
teachers	13,358	2.0	15,005	3.5
civil service officers & clerks	2549	0.4	2804	0.6
commercial clerks	305		7849	1.8
gen. shopkeepers	15,382	2.4	12,800	3.0
drapers	2648	0.4	4989	1.2
grocers	3629	0.6	2563	0.6
confectioners/ pastry-cooks	1118	0.2	1610	0.4
innkeeper/hotel/ lodging house	4592	0.7	4835	1.1
TOTAL	634,793		430,092	

Source: Census of Ireland, 1881–1911

The nearness of England and the ready access to English newspapers and magazines meant that some of the ideas which made service increasingly less attractive to English girls also affected their Irish counterparts. Given alternatives, as girls were in England, they became dissatisfied with the working conditions of servants, especially the long hours and the lack of freedom. Writing in 1903 Charles Booth noted that 'a very independent spirit is a marked characteristic of the lower classes of servants', and he added: 'to such as these the loss of independence which service entails becomes unbearable'.[27] Mrs J. Ramsay McDonald, honorary secretary of the Legal Committee of the Women's Industrial Council, giving evidence to the Royal Commission on the Poor Law and Relief of Distress, 1910, attributed the disinclination of girls to enter service in England as 'a question of social caste'. She said they did not want service when their friends worked in shops and factories.[28] Women in Ireland were affected by democratic ideas current in the USA and England, movements such as the emancipation of women were altering traditional ideas and so expectations rose without the means to satisfy them being available in the country.

Meanwhile employers were seeking solutions to what was known as 'the servant problem'. One method advocated was the use of 'lady helps'. This was first tried in England in the 1870s when needy gentlewomen were recruited as upper servants. It was not very successful, for, like governesses, lady helps belonged neither to the world of the servant nor of the employer and, where other servants were involved, they were often a cause of friction.[29] It was thought that many social difficulties would be solved if young ladies would agree to become lady helps in their own homes: 'families rich only in daughters will spare of their super-abundant "helps" to serve as upper servants in the houses of more wealthy people; and in those of the childless'.[30] The idea of the lady helps was revived in England in the early 1900s with the establishment of organizations such as the Guild of the Dames of the Household at Cheltenham in 1902, the Guild of Aids at Bath and the Central Bureau for the Employment of Women in London. Again this did not meet with much success.[31] Letters advocating the use of lady helps in Ireland and offering advice on training appeared in the 1890s.[32] One writer said that it was usually supposed that the lady help was needed in a large establishment where many servants were employed, but that many advantages would ensue if the lady help 'was willing to enter more humble families and to make herself generally useful'.[33] In 1908 an article in *The Lady of the House* suggested that ladies should train as dames of the household in Cheltenham, and stated that there were a number of Irish girls in training there and that it was possible to get suitable places in Ireland when finished. Details about applications, fees and duration of training – this could vary from two weeks for parlourmaids, to three months for cooks and children's nurses – were given. The Guild of the Dames of the Household also laid down conditions of employment.[34] The introduction of lady helps in Ireland probably met with even less success than in England. When they were mentioned in magazines it was usually with disparagement, they were described as being too much of the 'lady' and not enough of the 'help'.[35] This reflects the ambiguity of their position and differences in how they saw themselves and their employers saw them. Employers complained that these women were apt to remember what they used to be rather than their present circumstances.[36]

A more radical suggestion to alleviate servant shortages and servant discontent was to introduce central kitchens. A letter to *The Lady of the House* in 1896 advocated a culinary depot in each street where meals could be prepared; the menu would be sent around to each house in advance and orders taken. A secondary kitchen producing plain luncheons, and servants' and children's dinners was even envisaged. The writer hoped that the same type of competition which existed between shops and tradesmen would develop in this service.[37] The idea was revived many years later in an effort to apply the more efficient methods of industry to the organization of the home. This time it was linked with the employment of what was known as 'the eight-hour home assistant'. This person arrived in time to lay the table for breakfast, receive the hot cooked meal which had been ordered the previous day from the 'central' or 'neighbourhood' kitchen, make tea and toast and serve the meal, return the dishes to the container for collection and then proceed to do the other household chores. In order to cover the full day until after dinner, a shift system would be necessary. In a large house the employment of two assistants working together might be required. Lunch and dinner would be delivered hot, appetizing and ready to serve; savings from the elimination of waste and breakages were promised.[38] However attractive these ideas may have appeared to some at the time, they were never seriously entertained. They had been mooted in England at various times from the early 1890s but never really put into practice.[39]

The suggestions which do not appear to have been given serious consideration were firstly that housewives and other members of the family should do the housework themselves, and secondly, that greater use should be made of labour-saving appliances. These were the two methods by which, for most people, the 'servant problem' was eventually solved. Technological advances and new inventions did not affect the housewife until the first years of the 1900s and indeed did not affect many for several decades later.

In America, household guides at the turn of the century showed that technology had changed many household tasks. Middle-class apartments had central heating, hot water and modern appliances.[40] The iron was electrified in 1882, the sewing machine in 1889, and the stove in 1896.[41] These changes came more slowly in

Europe. It was indeed maintained that the presence of servants delayed the technical improvement of homes for many years.[42] Gas was first used to light the streets of Dublin on the 5 October 1825, its use was gradually adopted for lighting private houses.[43] Most people, however, continued to use candles and lamps until the advent of electric light many years later. In the middle of the nineteenth century a pamphlet prepared in England for the Alliance and Dublin Consumers' Gas Company described the first gas cooker:

By the aid of a simply constructed apparatus gas performs the respective processes of roasting, baking, frying, boiling, steaming etc. that cannot be attained by means of the common fire. Two or three days' experience are sufficient to enable servants to conduct any of the above mentioned operations with certainty as respect of time.[44]

This piece of 'simply constructed apparatus' did not appear in Dublin homes until the first decade of the new century. People living in the more prosperous areas of the city, such as Merrion Square, Northumberland Road, Highfield Road and Mountjoy Square, started to use gas for cooking, heating and water heating in 1907–8.[45] It is significant that when labour-saving appliances first appeared, servants were seen as the people who would use these devices.

In 1892 Dublin Corporation first supplied street lighting and offered current to citizens who wished to install electric lighting in their own homes. Previous to this private companies had supplied electricity for some street lighting in Dublin – in 1881 electric lighting was used in St Stephen's Green and Nassau Street. In 1903 the electricity works were moved from Fleet Street to the Pigeon House, where there was much greater capacity to generate electricity.[46] In 1904 there were only 650 consumers in Dublin and most of these were using electricity only for lighting or as power for industry.[47] There was an electrical exhibition in the Mansion House, Dublin, from 30 October to 4 November 1911, at which electric cookers, fires, hot plates and heaters for shaving water were exhibited. It is clear from the catalogue that these appliances were new to most people at the time.[48] By the 1920s no house was considered modern or properly equipped unless it had electric light, but it was only in the mid twenties that the public was beginning to realize the advantages of using electricity for cooking, heating, washing, ironing and vacuum cleaning.[49] In the years before the Shannon scheme was inaugurated, Ireland had by far the lowest consumption of electricity of any modern European country – 16 units per head of population. In 1923 there was a consumption of 26 units per head in Dublin as against 105 in Amsterdam. There were 40,000 houses in Dublin city and 13,000, less than one-third, had electricity installed. Only 23 per cent of people in Cork and 9 per cent of the population in Limerick had electricity. In the areas of the Free State where electricity was available, only 26 per cent of the people had it installed.[50] Ireland was slow to avail of the benefits of electricity and the wide range of appliances which electricity made possible. Of course labour-saving appliances appeared before the advent of gas and electricity. There were, for instance, hand-operated washing machines,[51] mechanical vacuum cleaners,[52] iceboxes, mangles and wringers, but they were probably used by very few people. It is reasonable to suspect that labour-saving appliances became popular in this country only when women had to do their own housework.

After the First World War in England a determined effort was made to force women into domestic service. If an unemployed woman was offered a job as a servant and she refused it, she lost the right to unemployment benefit. In 1919 650,000 women were unemployed, of whom only 500,000 were receiving unemployment benefit. The others who had refused domestic service were denied relief.[53] The government organized two programmes to train unemployed women as domestic servants and 11,388 were trained under these schemes.[54]

All efforts, however, in Ireland, England and elsewhere to halt the decline in domestic service failed and a trend which started in the 1880s continued inexorably and with increasing momentum during the following sixty to seventy years. The most surprising aspect of the decline and eventual demise of domestic service was that people did not seem to realize that it was going to happen. There was obviously an awareness of the decline, but all the proposed solutions – right up to the 1940s – were directed at rescuing an industry in difficulties, making it more attractive, more efficient, more in keeping with changing times. But it was not just a question of solving an economic problem, of improving the efficiency of an industry: domestic service was also part of the social fabric, a structure by which one group in society not only laboured on behalf of another group, but by their existence gave status and caste to their employers. The very titles 'master' and 'servant' defined not just economic relationships but also positions in society. In 1825 the Adams could say: 'no relations in society are so numerous and universal as those of masters and servants'.[55] This relationship continued to be important in the ordering of society for more than a hundred years. When change came, it came not for economic reasons alone, not just because other more attractive jobs became available – this was a factor but certainly not the dominant factor in Ireland. Change came because the inferior, dependent position of the servant became unacceptable in a more democratic world. The widening of women's horizons, ideals of equality and emancipation, which were strengthened by a world war, all affected a country which had close language and communication links with powerful neighbours. Ireland was unable to satisfy these aspirations and so thirty-five years and another world war passed, and thousands emigrated, before domestic service virtually ceased to exist.

— Appendix —

STUDY OF THE EMPLOYMENT OF DOMESTIC SERVANTS IN DUBLIN HOUSES IN 1911

This study was based on a sample of approximately 850 Dublin households in 1911. The rateable valuation of houses was used as the criterion of the social and economic status of the occupier. Samples of houses with rateable valuations of £10–£19, £20–£39, and £40 or over were chosen. It was considered very unlikely that any household with a rateable valuation of less than £10 would have a servant and this was borne out by the pilot study and also by the small number of households in the lowest group selected, £10–£19, in which servants were employed.

It was decided to select 250 houses with a rateable valuation (RV) of £20–£39, 250 with one of £40 or over (it was found that there was approximately equal representation of these RV groupings in Dublin city and the urban county districts) and 300 houses with a rateable valuation of £10–£19. This group was over-represented deliberately as a pilot study had shown that the number in this category employing a servant was small. An effort was made to have a fairly wide geographical coverage of Dublin city and the urban districts. The houses were selected randomly from *Thom's Directory* for 1911. Half of the houses were from the suburbs, Blackrock, Kingstown, Killiney, Pembroke, Rathmines and Rathgar where there was a high concentration of servants – one for every ten people. In Dublin city in 1911, there was one for every twenty-five of the population.[1] A sample of fifty-three prominent citizens was selected from *Thom's Directory* by choosing people who held important positions in the church and the government, administration and defence of the country, as well as some of the leading lawyers, doctors, educators and important businessmen. This ensured that some households with larger staffs would be included in the study. In all, 860 employers and 1038 servants – 970 women and 68 men – were involved in the study. Sixty country houses in Ireland were selected from a list of mansions in Ireland prepared for the House of Commons in 1906;[2] they were chosen to give a good coverage of the whole country.

Information on the households selected was obtained from the enumerators' returns for the 1911 census. This information was codified and the following data recorded:

1 sex of head of household
2 religion
3 social class
4 occupational class

113

5   occupation
6   income (if available)
7   rateable valuation of the house
8   location of house – for Dublin the street, for country house the province
9   number in household (excluding the servants)
10   number of children under 11 years of age
11   number of children of 11 years of age and over
12   children, or other members of the family, who were earning, other than the main breadwinner
13   women, other than the wife, not working outside the home
14   number of boarders kept
15   number of servants
16   number of male servants
17   male employers if single or widower
18   if head of country house was not at home
19   servants in country house away from home with employer

For each servant the following information was recorded:
1   sex
2   religion
3   literacy
4   age, in 5-year intervals
5   occupation as servant, e.g. general servant, butler, cook
6   marital status
7   place of birth – Dublin city or county, adjoining counties, rest of Leinster, Munster, Ulster, Connacht, GB, others, not known

Country houses – local (same county), adjoining county, elsewhere in Ireland, England & Wales, Scotland, abroad, not known

For the classification of the heads of households according to social standing and occupational class the method used by Guy Routh in *Occupation and Pay in Great Britain, 1906–1960*[3] was used, but adapted to suit Ireland in the early years of the century. As Guy Routh was only interested in pay and occupation, some self-employed people, proprietors and employers, were omitted; these have been put into the middle class and 'employers and proprietors' class. Owners of very large businesses were allocated to the upper-class and 'proprietors of large businesses'. People whose income was derived from property, annuities and investment were omitted from the Routh classification. For this study, people of independent means, or who were presumed to have independent means, were allocated to the upper or middle classes depending on the rateable valuation of the houses, and general factors such as the occupations of other family members. University professors and heads of colleges were allocated to the upper and higher professional classes, and teachers to the middle and lower professional classes.

APPENDIX

SOCIAL CLASS	OCCUPATIONAL CLASS
Upper	Independent means
	Higher professional
	Proprietors of large businesses
Middle	Lower professional
	Employers & proprietors
	Managers & administrators
	Independent means
Lower Middle	Clerical workers
	Foremen, supervisors, inspectors
	Skilled manual
Semi-skilled	Semi-skilled
Unskilled	Unskilled

The upper-class consisted only of the higher professions, owners of very large businesses and the wealthier of those with independent means. The extra information available on enumerators' returns allowed distinctions to be made between those of 'independent means' – 45 per cent of whom were put into the middle class.

One of the aims of this study was to compare the keeping of servants with the status and income of the head of household. For this reason social class as well as occupational class was important. While there are very close links between social class and occupational class they are not identical. Other factors such as education are taken into consideration when defining social class. Many of those who are considered semi-skilled from the occupational point of view are allocated to the lower middle class, examples of these are shop assistants, storekeepers, members of the armed forces, drivers of passenger and goods vehicles and most domestic servants. For this reason, while there are many semi-skilled workers in the sample, there are very few people in the semi-skilled social class. Also, there is no precise relationship between remuneration and social class. Lower professional people belong to the middle class but many earned less than skilled workers in the lower middle class.

It was found that the rateable valuation of a house was a good indicator of whether or not servants were likely to be employed; 96 per cent of houses with a valuation of £40 or over had servants, 69 per cent of those with a valuation of £20–£39 had servants employed. Rateable valuation was also a good indicator of the social class of the occupier.

While there was of course overlap between social class and houses of different rateable valuations, over 80 per cent of the lowest valuation houses were occupied by people belonging to the lower middle class; over 80 per cent of the £20–£39 houses were occupied by the middle and lower middle classes; while almost all houses with rateable valuations of £40 and over were occupied by the upper and middle classes (62.6 per cent were upper class).

Rateable valuation was also a good indication of occupational class. While there was of course overlap, the houses with the highest valuation had a very high proportion of heads with high-status occupations, 69 per cent of heads belonged to occupational class 1 and 26 per cent to occupational class 2. On the other hand, 60 per cent of those living in houses with a rateable valuation of £10–£19 belonged to occupational class 3 and 20 per cent to class 4.

A very close link was found between social class and the employment of servants; 98 of the upper-class employed servants, 71 per cent of the middle class and only 23 per cent of the lower middle class. All servants were employed by those three social classes.

FACTORS AFFECTING EMPLOYMENT OF SERVANT

Keeping of boarders
People who kept boarders were less likely to have servants than those who did not keep boarders. Those with a number of lodgers, four or more, did keep a servant. They probably considered it an occupation and usually described themselves as boarding-house keepers.

Children
People with young children were more likely to have servants than those without children. In large houses, where servants were employed anyway, it was found that households with young children had an average of 2.6 servants, those without young children had an average of 2.2 servants. In the homes of prominent citizens, those with young children employed an average of five servants, while those without young children had an average of 4.6 servants.

Presence of women relatives other than wives not working outside the home
In the lowest valuation houses, £10–£19, 78 per cent of houses had only wives at home – if other women lived there, they worked outside the home. Households with rateable valuation of £20–£39 and unemployed women relatives, were less likely to have servants than those in which the housewife had to do all the household work. In the large houses, RV of £40 or over, the presence or not of other women relatives did not affect the employment of servants.

One or more earner in the household
There was a very significant negative correlation between the employment of servants and the number of people earning and this was true in all categories of houses. Where there was only one earner, servants were more likely to be employed, and, apart from the smaller houses, the number of servants was greater.

TABLE 12

The percentage of employers who were Catholic, Protestant etc. according to RV of houses (number in brackets)

| RV/£ | RC | RELIGION | | | TOTAL |
		PROTESTANT	OTHER	UNKNOWN	
10–19	63 (22)	34 (12)		3 (1)	100 (35)
20–39	29 (51)	66 (115)	4 (7)	1 (2)	100 (175)
40 +	29 (69)	64 (153)	5 (12)	2 (5)	100 (239)
PROMINENT CITIZENS	28 (15)	68 (36)	2 (1)	2 (1)	100 (53)
TOTAL	(157)	(316)	(20)	(9)	(502)

116

TABLE 13
Percentage of RC and Protestant servants in different-sized houses
(number of servants in brackets)

RV/£	RELIGION		TOTAL
	RC	PROTESTANT	
10–19	89 (32)	11 (4)	100 (36)
20–39	89.7 (184)	10.3 (21)	100 (205)
40 +	76.5 (418)	23.5 (128)	100 (546)
PROMINENT CITIZENS	63 (160)	37 (94)	100 (254)

TABLE 14
Percentage of servants of different religious affiliations employed by Catholics and Protestants in Dublin houses in 1911 (number in brackets)

RELIGION OF EMPLOYERS		RELIGION OF SERVANTS			TOTAL
		RC	PROT.	OTHER	
RC	(157)	97 (297)	3 (8)	(1)	100 (306)
PROT.	(316)	67 (461)	32 (219)	1 (4)	100 (684)
OTHER	(20)	(29)	(11)		(40)
UNKNOWN	(9)	(14)	(5)		(19)
TOTAL	(502)	(801)	(243)	(5)	(1049)

TABLE 15
Percentage of servants in different age groups in small, medium and large houses
(number in brackets)

AGE GROUP	SMALL	SIZE OF HOUSE MEDIUM	LARGE	PROMINENT CITIZENS	TOTAL NO.
15–19	47 (17)	19 (39)	8 (43)	11.5 (29)	128
20–4	19 (7)	37 (76)	22 (119)	26 (66)	268
25–9	11 (4)	16 (32)	27 (147)	21 (53)	236
30–4	3 (1)	7 (14)	11 (59)	9.5 (24)	98
35–9		8 (16)	9.5 (52)	11 (28)	96
40–4	3 (1)	4 (8)	5 (30)	8 (21)	60
45–9		1.5 (3)	6 (33)	5 (13)	49
50–4	8 (3)	3 (6)	2.5 (14)	3.5 (9)	32
55–9		1.5 (3)	3 (18)	2.5 (6)	27
60–4	3 (1)	1 (2)	4 (20)	1 (3)	26
65 +	6 (2)	2 (4)	2 (11)	1 (2)	19
TOTAL	100 (36)	100 (203)	100 (546)	100 (254)	1039

TABLE 16
Percentage of servants in different age groups in Dublin houses and in country houses (number in brackets)

SERVANTS AGE GROUP	HOUSES		COUNTRY HOUSES		TOTAL	
15–19	12	(128)	18	(104)	14	(232)
20–4	26	(268)	30	(170)	27	(438)
25–9	23	(236)	17	(93)	21	(329)
30–4	9	(98)	12	(65)	10	(163)
35–9	9	(96)	9	(50)	9	(146)
40–4	6	(60)	5	(28)	5	(88)
45–9	5	(49)	4	(25)	5	(74)
50–4	3	(32)	2	(10)	3	(42)
55–9	3	(27)	1	(7)	2	(34)
60–4	2	(26)	2	(9)	2	(35)
65 +	2	(19)			1	(19)
TOTAL	100	(1039)	100	(561)	100	(1600)

TABLE 17
Percentage of female servants single, married and widowed in different age groups in Dublin houses (number in brackets)

AGE GROUP	SINGLE		MARRIED		WIDOWED		TOTAL	
15–19	98.4	(123)	1.6	(2)			100	(125)
20–4	100	(252)					100	(252)
25–9	97.7	(217)	1.4	(3)	0.9	(2)	100	(222)
30–4	95.4	(82)	2.3	(2)	2.3	(2)	100	(86)
35–9	80.5	(74)	4.3	(4)	15.2	(14)	100	(92)
40–4	78.1	(43)	5.5	(3)	16.4	(9)	100	(55)
45–9	74.4	(32)			25.6	(11)	100	(43)
50–4	70.4	(19)	7.4	(2)	22.2	(6)	100	(27)
55–9	74	(17)	4.3	(1)	21.7	(5)	100	(23)
60–4	66.7	(18)	3.7	(1)	29.6	(8)	100	(27)
65 +	66.7	(12)			33.3	(6)	100	(18)
TOTAL	91.6	(889)	1.9	(18)	6.5	(63)	100	(970)

APPENDIX

TABLE 18
Percentage of male servants single, married and widowed in different age groups in Dublin houses (number in brackets)

AGE GROUP	SINGLE		MARRIED		WIDOWED		TOTAL	
15–19	100	(5)					100	(5)
20–4	100	(17)					100	(17)
25–9	85.7	(12)	14.3	(2)			100	(14)
30–4	55.6	(5)	44.4	(4)			100	(9)
35–9	80	(4)	20	(1)			100	(5)
40–4	50	(2)	50	(2)			100	(4)
45–9	20	(1)	60	(3)	20	(1)	100	(5)
50–4	50	(2)	25	(1)	25	(1)	100	(4)
55–9			50	(2)	50	(2)	100	(4)
65 +					100	(1)	100	(1)
TOTAL	70.6	(48)	22	(15)	7.4	(5)	100	(68)

TABLE 19
Percentage of female servants single, married and widowed, in different age groups in country houses (number in brackets)

AGE GROUP	SINGLE		MARRIED		WIDOWED		TOTAL	
15–19	100	(73)					100	(73)
20–4	100	(122)					100	(122)
25–9	100	(66)					100	(66)
30–4	98	(50)			2	(1)	100	(51)
35–9	88	(37)	7	(3)	5	(2)	100	(42)
40–4	87	(20)			13	(3)	100	(23)
45–9	70.6	(12)	11.8	(2)	17.6	(3)	100	(17)
50–4	100	(7)					100	(7)
55–9	40	(2)			60	(3)	100	(5)
60–4	100	(3)					100	(3)
65 +	50	(2)	25	(1)	25	(1)	100	(4)
TOTAL	95.5	(394)	1.5	(6)	3	(13)	100	(413)

TABLE 20
Percentage of male servants single, married and widowed, in different age groups in country houses (number in brackets)

AGE GROUP	SINGLE		MARRIED		WIDOWED		TOTAL	
15–19	100	(31)					100	(31)
20–4	98	(46)	2	(1)			100	(47)
25–9	93	(26)	7	(2)			100	(28)
30–4	84.6	(11)	15.4	(2)			100	(13)
35–9	62.5	(5)	37.5	(3)			100	(8)
40–4	80	(4)	20	(1)			100	(5)
45–9	43	(3)	43	(3)	14	(1)	100	(7)
50–4	33.3	(1)	66.7	(2)			100	(3)
55–9			50	(1)	50	(1)	100	(2)
60–4			100	(3)			100	(3)
65 +			100	(1)			100	(1)
TOTAL	86	(127)	13	(19)	1	(2)	100	(148)

TABLE 21
Birthplace of servants, according to the size of house, in percentages (number in brackets)

PROM. BIRTHPLACE CITIZENS	RV			HOM
	£10–£19	£20–£39	£40 +	
Dublin city & county	57 (20)	39 (80)	25 (138)	22 (54)
rest Leinster	17 (6)	38 (78)	46 (250)	41 (101)
other three provinces	17 (6)	17 (35)	22 (118)	25 (64)
Great Britain	9 (3)	6 (12)	5 (30)	11 (27)
others		(1)	2 (10)	1 (3)
TOTAL	100 (35)	100 (206)	100 (546)	100 (249)

APPENDIX

TABLE 22
Birthplace of servants in Dublin houses in percentages and numbers

BIRTHPLACE	PERCENTAGE	NUMBER
Dublin city	15	152
Dublin county	13	140
Meath, Wicklow, Kildare	21	217
rest of Leinster	21	218
Munster	8	84
Ulster	7.5	79
Connaught	6	60
Great Britain	7	72
other countries	1	10
unspecified	0.5	4
TOTAL	100	1036

APPENDIX

TABLE 23
Servants – occupations and numbers in Dublin houses

OCCUPATION	1	2	3	4	5	6	7	8	9	10	TOTAL
Female											
general servant	145	22	3	2	2	1					175
not specified	71	48	17	16	13	13	1	5	1		185
housemaid	1	37	38	25	18	17	5	2	2	7	152
parlourmaid		20	28	17	10	9	2			2	88
house/parlour	1	21	4	2		1					29
housekeeper	4	2	2	4	2		1			1	16
cook	19	81	51	25	15	14	3	1	1	3	213
kitchen-maid		1	1	3	9	9	2	1	1	3	30
scullery maid									1	3	4
laundry maid										2	2
nurse/children's maid	2	21	18	13	7	5	1	1		2	70
lady's maid			2	3	3	3			1	3	15
other		1			1						2
Male											
general man			2								2
not specified						1					1
butler		2	2	3	2	4	2	1	1	1	18
footman			1			3	1	1	1	2	9
house steward					1						1
pantry/hallboy						1		1	1		3
valet										1	1
chef				1							1
coachman/chauffeur			2	4	5	7	2	2			22
groom						1	3		1		5
gardener		2	1	1							4
TOTAL											1048
NUMBER OF HOUSEHOLDS	243	129	57	30	18	15	3	2	1	3	501

APPENDIX

TABLE 24
Servants – occupations and numbers in country houses

OCCUPATION	3	4	5	6	7	8	9	10	11	12	13	14	15	16	17	18	19	TOTAL
Female																		
housemaid		3	5	9	11	9	12	10	8	18	13	3	6	7	3	8	4	129
parlourmaid		2					2	2						2				8
house/parlour	1	1																2
housekeeper	1				4	2	1	1		5	2	1		1		2	1	21
cook		4	2	6	3	2	5	4	3	5	3	1	2	2	1	2	1	46
kitchen-maid		2		6	3	1	7	3	3	7	5	1	2	3	2	4	2	51
scullery maid				1	3		1	3	2	5	2	1	1	1		1		21
laundry maid				1		2	1	1	2	8		2	2	2	2	1		24
dairy maid							1	1		2	1	1		1		1		8
still-room maid					1					1			1			2		5
lady's maid			1	2	2		3	1	3	4	4	1	3	2	1	4	1	32
nurse						2	6	5		4	7		3	2	4	2	2	37
general servant		1			6	1								1				9
not specified/other		1			7		8		2		1				1			20
Male																		
steward house/estate					1	1				1								3
butler		1	1	3	2	3	3	3	3	4	3	1	2	1		1	1	32
under butler															1			1
footman			1	4	1	3	7	4	3	8	7	2	3	2	2	5	2	54
hallboy				1	1		1	1	1	3	2		2	1		1	1	15
valet							1	1		1							1	4
general man			2	1					1	1			1			1	1	8
coachman/chauffeur				1	1				1	2			1		1			7
groom/stableman	1			1				4			4			1	3			14
gardener		1									1							2
other											1	1		1			2	5
TOTAL																		558
NUMBER OF BIG HOUSES	1	4	2	6	6	4	7	4	3	7	4	1	2	2	1	2	1	57

— Notes —

INTRODUCTION

1 Census of Ireland, 1881, 1891, 1901, 1911.
2 Pamela Horn, *The Rise and Fall of the Victorian Servant* (London & New York 1975), p.159.
3 Ministry of reconstruction. Report of the Women's Advisory Committee on the domestic service problem, together with reports by sub-committees on training, machinery of distribution, organization and conditions, p.31 [Cmd 67], HC1919, XXIX, 37.
4 Former servant at Tara to author, 12 April 1980.
5 Former servant, Farrell Street, Kells, to author, 12 March 1980.
6 Report of domestic service sub-committee on training, p.11–17.
7 Samuel and Sarah Adams, *The Complete Servant* (Lewes 1989), p.20.

ONE

1 National Archives, Census of Ireland., 1911, Dublin 34/35 (henceforward Nat. Arch., Cen. Ire.; references to census re-turns are all to A form).
2 *Ibid.*
3 Wages of domestic servants. Board of Trade (labour department). Report by Miss Collet on the money wages of indoor domestic servants, p.14 [C9346], HC1899, XCII, 22.
4 Charles Booth, *Life and Labour in London* (London & New York 1903), p.212.
5 This is also the figure suggested in England by a number of writers: Isabella Beeton, *The Book of Household Management* (London 1892), p.6; Patricia Branca, *The Silent Sisterhood: Middle-Class Women in the Victorian Home* (London 1975), p.27; Pamela Horn, *Rise and Fall*, p.24; Herman Muthesius, *The English House* (London 1979), p.70.
6 Report of the Select Committee on Post-Office Servants (wages and conditions of employment), pp.707, 710, HC1913 (268) XI, vol.1: minutes of evidence, 8 May 1912 to 27 November 1912 (268), HC1913, XI, pp.707, 710.
7 Howard H. Hely, ' The Middle Class' in *The Irish Homestead*, XXII, no.31 (31 July 1915), p.503.
8 Former employer in Eglinton Park, Dún Laoghaire, to author, 18 April 1980.
9 Mona Hearn, 'Domestic Servants in Dublin, 1880–1920', unpublished Ph.D. thesis, Trinity College Dublin, 1984.
10 Nat. Arch., Cen. Ire., 1911, Dublin 75–3.
11 Nat. Arch., Cen. Ire., 1911, Dublin 58–83.
12 Elizabeth Smith, *Irish Journals, 1840–1850*, David Thompson & Moyra

McGusty (eds), (Oxford 1980), p.210.

13 Census of Ireland, 1911.
14 Mary E. Daly, *Dublin, the Deposed Capital* (Cork 1984), pp.124–5.
15 C.S. Andrews, *Dublin Made Me* (Dublin & Cork 1979), p.43.
16 R.M. Fox, *Louie Bennett* (Dublin 1957), p.13.
17 See advertisements for servants in the 1880s, e.g. *The Irish Times (IT)*, 9 & 10 January, 4 & 6 June 1883. Golden Bridge Industrial School Register, no.1, d–400, Mary Dowdall, a 'thoro servant' in 1886, p.34. The origin of the word is not clear. Horn mentions a 'through servant', *Rise and Fall*, p.111 – possibly meaning one who did all the different categories of work in a house.
18 In 'Domestic Servants in Dublin', in which the suburbs and the servant-keeping classes were over-represented and very low rateable valuation houses, which might have had a maid, were omitted, 63 per cent of employers had only one servant. It is not unreasonable to expect that the percentage for the whole city was considerably higher.
19 Beeton, *Book of Household Management*, p.1180.
20 Nat. Arch., Cen. Ire., 1911, Dublin 61/88.
21 Booth, *Life and Labour*, p.218.
22 Andrews, *Dublin Made Me*, pp.10, 11.
23 Census of Ireland, 1911.
24 *Ibid.*, 1891, 1911.
25 Smith, *Irish Journals*, p.214.
26 Male servants, hearths and windows in Castletown House for purpose of tax (TCD, Ms 3969).
27 Horn, *Rise and Fall*, pp.9–10.
28 Booth, *Life and Labour*, p.227.
29 Lockwood Davidoff, 'Domestic Service and the Working-Class Cycle' in *Society for the Study of Labour History (SSLH)*, Bulletin no.26 (Spring 1977), p.10.
30 Census of Ireland, 1911.
31 *Ibid.*, 1881, 1891, 1901, 1911.
32 There is an example of this in Castletown House.
33 This is seen from newspaper advertisements and from enumerators' returns for the 1911 census.
34 Hearn, 'Domestic Servants in Dublin'. See Table 14, p.116.
35 Census of Ireland, 1911.
36 Former employer in Eglinton Park, Dún Laoghaire, to author, 18 April 1980.
37 43 per cent of male servants working in Dublin were Protestants as against 22 per cent of female servants, Hearn, 'Domestic Servants in Dublin'. Mary Daly also comments on the high percentage of male Church of Ireland servants in Dublin; Daly, *Dublin, the Deposed Capital*, p.124.
38 Terence de Vere White, *The Anglo Irish* (London 1972), p.181.
39 Census of Ireland, 1911.
40 'Employers preferred their servants to be single, and even a diligent married man might have difficulty in securing a place'; Horn, *Rise and Fall*, p.40.
41 Hearn, 'Domestic Servants in Dublin'. See Table 17, p.117.

42 Census of Ireland, 1911.
43 Hearn, 'Domestic Servants in Dublin'. See Table 23, p.121.
44 This is also stressed by many writers; McBride, *Domestic Revolution*, pp.56, 90; David Katzman, *Seven Days a Week* (New York & Oxford 1978), p.269; L. Davidoff and R. Hawthorn, *A Day in the Life of a Victorian Domestic Servant* (London 1976), p.88.
45 Board of Trade – Employment of Women (Labour Department). Report by Miss Collet on the statistics of employment of women and girls, p.29, [c7564], HC1894, LXXXI, pt. II, 881.
46 'This meant that you could not ask anyone in' (former servant at Dublin Central Mission, Marlborough Place, to author, 12 March 1980).
47 *The Freeman's Journal* (*FJ*), 5 October 1880, p.2.
48 A former employer said that she told her servants to tell boyfriends that they were housekeepers (employer at Eglinton Park to author, 18 April 1980).
49 McBride pointed out that servants tended to marry late, when they had an opportunity to save, but that this was more noticeable in France than in England because of its agricultural traditions and the greater importance of dowries; McBride, *Domestic Revolution*, p.88.
50 Katzman, *Seven Days*, p.69.
51 Hearn, 'Domestic Servants in Dublin'. See Table 22, p.119.
52 Daly, *Dublin, the Deposed Capital*, pp.138, 142.
53 This also occured in Britain and France: McBride stated that: 'London between 1851 and 1871 drew 60 per cent of its servants from outside the city. In fact servants demonstrated consistently higher geographical mobility than any other job category: in France, in 1901, 48 per cent of servants were working outside their natal departments while only 30 per cent of the industrial workers were' (*Domestic Revolution*, p.35).
54 Hearn, 'Domestic Servants in Dublin'. See Table 21, p.119.
55 Katzman, *Seven Days*, p.250.
56 A. Egmont Hake, *Suffering London* (London 1892), p.72.
57 Charlotte Deane, 'Domestic Service as a Profession' in *The New Ireland Review*, XIX, June 1903, p.221.
58 Violet M. Firth, *The Psychology of the Servant Problem* (London 1925), p.83.
59 Hake, *Suffering London*, p.70.
60 McBride, *Domestic Revolution*, pp.32–3.
61 Reminiscences of former servants and employers. Mss sources relating to 'big houses' in Ireland.
62 McBride, *Domestic Revolution*, p.100.
63 Merlin Waterson, *The Servants' Hall: A Domestic History of Erddig* (London 1980), p.110.
64 Royal Commission on Poor Law and Relief of Distress. Appendix, volume VIII. Minutes of Evidence (123rd to 138th days) with Appendix. This volume contains the oral and written evidence of witnesses relating, chiefly, to the subject of 'unemployment', p.210 [Cd 5066], HC1910, XLVIII, 210.
65 Smith, *Irish Journals*, p.221.
66 *Ibid.*, p.253.
67 James Plunkett, *Strumpet City* (London 1969), pp.65–7, 72.

68 Hake, *Suffering London*, p.68.
69 Clonbrock Papers (Ms 19568, entries for 31 May 1909 and 8 May 1910).
70 In Fond Remembrance: Headstone Inscriptions from St Columbas, Graveyard, no.2. Fingall Heritage Group, pp.8, 14.
71 Katherine Everett, *Bricks and Flowers* (London 1953), p.164.
72 Letters exchanged between the Lemon family and Biddy in possession of Biddy's descendant.
73 Former employer, Dublin, to author, 10 January 1980.
74 *IT*, 8 January 1895, 19 March 1901, p.2.
75 *IT*, 8 January 1907, p.2.
76 *FJ*, 19 January 1892, p.1.
77 Derek Hudson, *Munby – Man of Two Worlds. The Life and Diaries of Arthur J. Munby, 1828–1910* (London 1972) p.437.
78 *Ibid.*, p.71.
79 *Ibid.*, p.115.
80 Rose Mary Crawshay, *Domestic Service for Gentlewomen: A Record of Experience and Success* (pamphlet 1896), pp.15–43.
81 Letters to 'The Women's Parliament' in *The Lady of the House* (15 June 1896), p.22.
82 Pamela Hinkson, *Seventy Years Young: Memories of Elizabeth, Countess of Fingall* (The Lilliput Press: Dublin 1991), p.159.
83 Letters to 'The Women's Parliament' in *The Lady of the House* (15 June 1896), p.22.
84 From former servant at Emly, Co. Tipperary, to author, 28 March 1980.
85 From former employers at Leenane, Lockanash, Trim, to author, 17 May 1980, and at Eglinton Park on 18 April 1980.
86 From former servant 'Kathleen' to author, no address, no date.
87 From former servant at Millmount, Mullingar, to author, 10 October 1980.
88 Patrick Campbell, 'A man from the Croaghs Remembers' in *Donegal Annual*, vol.8, no.1, 1969, p.113.
89 Letters to 'The Women's Parliament' in *The Lady of the House*, 31st year (15 December 1920), p.20.

TWO

1 Six randomly selected copies of the *FJ* for the second half of 1880 showed that an average of 33 servants and 7 employers used the paper daily.
2 On 19 January 1904 4 housekeepers, 4 ladies' maids, 31 cooks, 1 cook/housekeeper, 30 housemaids and parlourmaids, 2 sewing maids, 1 maid, 35 general servants, 1 scullery maid, 1 kitchen-maid. 1 washing woman, 3 butler/valets, 9 coachmen, 6 groom/coachmen, 5 footmen, 3 grooms, 1 pantryman, 1 caretaker and 6 general men sought situations in *IT*.
3 Out of 1219 advertisements appearing in *The Freeman's Journal* between 1880 and 1913, only 31 mentioned religion, and only one of them was Church of Ireland.
4 *IT*, 19 March 1901, p.2.
5 *IT*, 1 July 1909, p.2.
6 *FJ*, 16 Nov. 1880.
7 Mostyn M. Bird, *Woman at Work* (London 1911), p.114.

8   Horn, *Rise and Fall*, p.40.
9   Katzman, *Seven Days*, p.104.
10 Minutes of evidence with appendices taken before group 'C' (textile, clothing, chemical, building and miscellaneous trades) of the Royal Commission on Labour. Evidence Mr G.W. Greenman, *London Domestic Servants' Union*, pp.445–6 [C 6894–IX], HC1893–4, XXXIV, 459–60.
11 Report from the Select Committee of the House of Lords on the law relating to the protection of young girls; together with the proceedings of the committee, minutes of evidence and appendix, pp.80, 90–1, HC1881 (448), IX, 440, 450–1.
12 *Ibid.*, p.84/444.
13 McBride, *Domestic Revolution*, p.77.
14 Public Health Acts Amendment Act, 1907.
15 Reports and Printed Documents of the Corporation of Dublin (RPDCD), vol.II, pp.481–5. The Public Health Acts Amendment Act, 1907. Bye-laws made by the Lord Mayor, Aldermen and Burgesses of Dublin.
16 RPDCD, Minutes of the Municipal Council of the City of Dublin 1913, pp.403–4; 1914, p.130.
17 RPDCD, Report of the Public Health Committee, 1912, vol.II, no.167, pp.200–1.
18 *Ibid.*, 1913, vol.1, no.28, p.220.
19 *Ibid.*, 1912, vol.II, no.167, p.502.
20 *Ibid.*, 1912, vol.II, no.167, p.201.
21 Correspondence between Mr M.J. Byrne, secretary, Regular Hotel and Club Workers' International Union, 16 Crampton Court, Dublin, and the Chief Secretary's Office. Letter from Mr Byrne to Rt Hon. Augustine Birrell on 19 March 1913 (file no.14794, Regular Hotel Workers' Union [M.J. Byrne]. Supervision of servants' registries, Sec. 85, Public Health Amendment Act, 1907. Transferred from SPOI to the Minister for Justice's Office in 1925. Made available to author at Nat. Arch.).
22 Girls Friendly Society (GFS) Report, 1909, p.25.
23 From former servants to author, one seen at the Old Folks' Association in Dún Laoghaire, 15 October 1980, the other at the Coast Road, Malahide, 1 May 1980. Minutes of evidence to Royal Commission on Labour, p.446 [C6894–IX], HC1893–4, XXIV, 460.
24 Mss of country houses, e.g. Clonbrock Papers (Ms 19567, entries for January and February 1909).
25 A former servant described 'the comfortable flagged kitchen' in an apartment owned by an agency in Holles St, where she stayed while waiting to be placed (from former servant living in Leighton Rd, Crumlin, to author, 23 March 1980). Advertisement from agency in *IT* on 25 January 1910, p.2, that lodgings at 2/6 a week were available. In Mrs Hunt's agency in London, girls slept in an attic while they waited for a 'situation' (Horn, *Rise and Fall*, p.41).
26 Frank O'Connor, *An Only Child* (Pan Books: London 1970), pp.48–9.
27 Placement book at Convent of Mercy, Lower Baggot St, Dublin.
28 GFS Minute Book, entry for October 1878. Associates who obtained a servant paid 1/-, others paid 2/6.

29   GFS Reports, 1879–82, pp.3, 4, 9.
30   GFS Minute Book, 21 Oct. 1878.
31   GFS Report, 1899, p.10.
32   *Ibid.*, 1900, p.23.
33   *Ibid.*, 1898, p.20.
34   *Ibid.*, 1898, p.18.
35   *Ibid.*, 1909, p.24.
36   L. McGlynn, 'Market for youth' in the *Irish Press* (27 November 1937); 'Observer Says' in the *Irish Press* (26 November 1943), describing 'rabble day' or hiring fairs in Derry, Strabane and Letterkenny, p.3; Michael Murphy, 'Open Air Labour Exchanges' in the *Times Pictorial* (11 November 1944), p.3; 'Hiring Fairs at Eyre Square, Galway and Athenry' in the *Sunday Press* (13 November 1949), p.4.
37   Department of Agriculture and Technical Instruction (DATI); Agricultural statistics of Ireland with detailed report for the year 1906, p.154 [Cd 3791], HC1908, CXXI, 782.
38   Sean McGrath, 35 Moore St, Kilrush, Co. Clare (Folklore Dept, UCD, Ms 1391, p.241). A lady who wrote to the author had a friend who got a job as general servant at a hiring fair in Donegal in the 1920s (anon. letter from Donegal). A former servant obtained his first situations at fairs in the 1920s. He said: 'In 1924 domestic servants and agricultural labourers were more or less one and the same thing' (former servant from Emly to author, 16 April 1980).
39   Paddy the Cope, *My Story* (Dungloe n.d.), p.8.
40   Patrick MacGill, *Children of the Dead End* (London 1914), p.31.
41   Michael Murphy, 'Open Air Labour Exchanges', p.3.
42   Beeton, *Household Management* (new edn, London 1923), p.1520; McBride, *Domestic Revolution*, p.73.
43   Character Note: A bill to make compulsory the giving of character notes, 1911, [Bill 167], p.1, HC1911, i, 213. Horn, *Rise and Fall*, p.46.
44   McBride, *Domestic Revolution*, p.73.
45   Margaret Powell, *Below Stairs* (London 1968), pp.124, 139. Another former servant was refused a reference by a mistress who did not want to lose her. She finally got one (former servant, Crumlin, to author, 23 March 1980). Another servant said that if one asked for a rise or complained, one could be asked to leave without a reference (former servant, B.D., to author, no date).
46   GFS Reports, 1879–92, p.8.
47   Orphan, anon., to author. Address unknown.
48   *FJ*, 16 November 1880.
49   Beeton, *Book of Household Management*, p.57.
50   Horn, *Rise and Fall*, p.45.
51   McBride, *Domestic Revolution*, p.73.
52   A bill 'to make it compulsory upon employers to supply a Reference Note to a person leaving their employment and deserving one', Horn, *Rise and Fall*, p.46.
53   Molly Keane, *Good Behaviour* (London 1981), p.13.
54   A letter from a former servant said: 'Madam could put whatever she liked

into a reference – could say you were a poor worker or had got careless or broke too many dishes. It used to puzzle me how someone could suit for 5 or 6 years and overnight become unsatisfactory' (anon. letter to author from Surrey, no date).

55   Beeton, *Household Management*, p.1520.
56   A former servant said that employers 'would give one reference and say something else behind your back' (former lady's maid to author at Nutly Park on 7 May 1980).
57   Beeton, *Household Management*, p.1520.
58   'Draft Code of the Byelaws' enclosed with a letter from Mr J. Byrne, Secretary of the Regular Hotel Workers' Union, to the Chief Secretary on 19 March 1913 (Nat. Arch., File no.14794).
59   Report of sub-committee on training, 1919, p.11/17.
60   Former servant at Tara to author, 12 April 1980.
61   Flora Thompson, *Lark Rise to Candleford* (London 1973), p.165. Horn, *Rise and Fall*, pp.33–4.
62   Report of Commission on Vocational Organization (Dublin 1943), p.282.
63   'The bulk of domestic servants no doubt obtain such training as may be from the mistress, or in large households, from the upper servants under whom they work.' Women's Advisory Committee, report of sub-committee on training, 1919, p.11/17.
64   Report by Miss Collet on the money wages, p.15/23.
65   McBride, *Domestic Revolution*, pp.84–5.
66   Katzman, *Seven Days*, p.136.
67   Firth, *Psychology of the Servant Problem*, p.42–3. Also report of the sub-committee on training, 1919, p.11/17.
68   'A Women Worker', 'Household hints' in *The Irish Homestead*, VIII, no.4 (Sat. 25 January 1902), p.74.
69   From former servant at Cabra, Thurles, to author, 27 February 1980.
70   Report of sub-committee on training, 1919, p.11/17.
71   Agriculture and Technical Instruction (Ireland) Act, 1899 (62 & 63 Vict., C50) established department of agriculture and technical instruction, and consultative council of agriculture including representatives of county councils.
72   Technical Instruction Act, 1889.
73   *The Irish Homestead*, VIII, no.25 (21 June 1902), p.479 and Vol.IX, no.13 (28 March 1903), p.260.
74   'Curriculum of City Schools' in the *Irish Independent*, 1 August 1903. 'Scripto', 'What is Being Done for Women's Advancement at the City of Dublin Technical Schools?' in *The Lady of the House* (14 November 1903), p.7.
75   'Housekeeping Instruction – a Suggestion by a Woman Worker' in *The Irish Homestead*, IV, no.169 (28 May 1898), p.460.
76   Report of the Commission on Technical Education, 1927, pp.16–7.
77   Report of Commission on Vocational Organization, p.282.
78   Evidence to the Commission on Vocational Organization (NL, vol.4, p.1311, par. 8288).
79   Others were at Dundrum, Dunmanway, Moate and Stradbally. Report of the Commission on Technical Education, 1927, p.34.

80 Deane, 'Domestic Service as a Profession', pp.219–26.
81 DATI, Twelfth annual general report for 1911–12, p.142 [Cd 6647], HC1912–13, XII, 672. Interview with Mrs K. Hickey, Roslea, Spencer Villas, Glenageary, former instructress in the school, on 6 May 1980.
82 GFS Report for 1894, p.19.
83 DATI, Third annual general report, pp.87–8/527–8.
84 Louise Kenny, 'A new Irish school of housewifery' in The Irish Homestead, XI, no.12 (25 March 1905), pp.240–1.
85 DATI, Ninth annual general report for 1908–9, p.116 [Cd 5128], HC1910, VIII, 738.
86 Caption on the billhead for the House of Mercy Laundry, Lower Baggot St, in 1840.
87 Interview with Sr de Lourdes in the Convent of Mercy, Baggot St, 21 April 1980.
88 Register of the House of Mercy, at Lower Baggot St, Dublin.
89 GFS Reports 1905, p.25; 1906, p.17; 1908, p.15.
90 Minutes of the GFS, 1 February 1913. Letter from Rev. T. O'Morchoe.
91 Eighteenth report of the inspector of reformatory and industrial schools of Ireland, p.26 [C 2692], HC1880, XXXVII, 397.
92 Robert F. Clokey, 'Irish Emigration from Workhouses' in Journal of the Statistical and Social Society of Ireland, III (1861–3), Part XXIV, IV, p.424.
93 Ibid.; Mark S. O'Shaughnessy, 'Some Remarks upon Mrs Hannah Archer's Scheme for Befriending Orphan Pauper Girls', Part XX, VI, pp.144–5. Mrs Hannah Archer, Kingsdowne House, Stratton St, Margaret, Wilts., had written about her scheme in Journal of the Workhouse Visiting Society in January 1862.
94 Florence Davenport-Hill, Children of the State (2nd edn, London & New York 1889), pp.23–5.
95 Ibid., pp.25–39.
96 Poor Law Union and Lunacy Inquiry Commission (Ireland). Report and evidence with appendices pp.191–218 [C 2239], HC1878–9, XXXI, 305–32.
97 Ibid., p.lviii/66.
98 Annual report of the local government board for Ireland being the eighth report under the Local Government (Ireland) Act, p.11 [C 2603], HC1880, XXVIII, 61.
99 Fifteenth annual report, p.94 [C 5124], HC1887, XXXVII, 106.
100 Twentieth annual report, pp.114–5 [C 6801], HC1892, XXXIX, 126–7.
101 Report of the Royal Commission on Poor Law and Relief of Distress, p.82 [Cd 4630], HC1909, XXXVIII, 88.
102 Joseph Robins, The Lost Children: A Study of Charity Children in Ireland, 1700–1900 (Dublin 1980), pp.275–6, 282, 305.
103 62 out of 78 reformatories and industrial schools were run by religious. Twenty-eighth report of the inspector, p.11 [C 6168], HC1890, XXXVIII, 483. Golden Bridge Industrial School Register, 401–701, shows that girls kept in touch with the nuns, e.g. no.417.
104 Eighteenth report of the inspector, Appendix VI, pp.110–11/482–3 [C 2692], HC1880, XXXVII, 397.
105 Ibid., pp.25–71/397–443. Detailed reports for reformatories and industrial

schools, pp.33–105/405–77.
106 Twenty-third report of the inspector, p.7/781.
107 Thirty-eighth report of the inspector, p.17 [Cd 345], HC1900, XLIII, 745.
108 Forty-second report of the inspector, p.17 [Cd 2257], HC1905, XXXVIII, 697.
109 *Ibid.*, p.19/699.
110 *Ibid.*, pp.20–1/700–1. Details of the syllabus pp.21–8/701–8.
111 Forty-fourth report of the inspector, p.17 [Cd 3146], HC1906, LIV, 225.
112 *Ibid.*, p.11/219.
113 Fifty-first report of the inspector, p.19 [Cd 7081], HC1914, XLVII, 511.
114 *Ibid.*, pp.33, 69–70/525, 561–2.
115 Fifty-seventh report of the inspector, p.16 [Cmd 571], HC1920, XXV, 16.
116 *Ibid.*, pp.12–13.
117 Poor Law Union (Ireland), 1879, pp.305–32. Book of discharges of juvenile offenders in St Joseph's Reformatory, High Park, Dublin. Book of discharges in Industrial School for Roman Catholic Girls in Golden Bridge, Dublin.
118 24 out of 544 girls discharged from industrial schools in 1879 emigrated (Eighteenth report of the inspector, p.15/387); 65 out of 569 discharged in 1883 emigrated (Twenty-third report of the inspector, p.17/791); 53 out of 708 emigrated in 1889 (Twenty-eighth report of the inspector, p.6/478).
119 Eighteenth report of the inspector, p.9/381.
120 Forty-eighth report of the inspector, p.14 [Cd 5318], HC1910, LVIII/14 and Fifty-first report of the inspector, p.14/506.
121 Book of discharges of juvenile offenders in St Joseph's Reformatory, High Park, Dublin.
122 Book of discharges in Industrial School, Golden Bridge, Dublin.
123 Industrial School, Golden Bridge, Registers, no.1–400, 401–700, 701–1011.
124 McBride, *Domestic Revolution*, pp.84–5.
125 Report of the sub-committee on training, 1919, p.14/20.
126 'Scripto', 'What is Being done...?' in *The Lady of the House*, p.8; letter from K. Ferguson in *The Irish Homestead*, IX, no.51 (19 Dec. 1903), p.1039; 'The Eight-Hour Home Assistant', in *The Lady of the House*, 30th year (14 June 1919), p.4.
127 Katzman, *Seven Days*, pp. 136–7, 244.
128 Horace Plunkett, *Ireland in the New Century* (Dublin 1983), p.273.

THREE
1 Former servant, Millmount, Mullingar, to author, 10 Oct. 1980.
2 *FJ*, 22 January 1889, p.2; 19 January 1892, p.2; 16 January 1894, p.8.
3 A general servant, aged fourteen, was paid £3.18.0. in 1902 (former servant in Old Folks Association, Dún Laoghaire, to author, 15 October 1980). An orphan, aged fourteen, was paid £4 a year in a doctor's house in the west of Ireland in 1936 (former servant, 'Kathleen', to author in 1980).
4 Poor Law Union (Ireland). 1879, p.199.
5 Folklore Department, UCD, Ms 462, p.275.
6 *Ibid.*, vol.172, p.82.
7 Agricultural Statistics of Ireland for 1906, p.158/786. Former farm servant

from Emly to author, 16 April 1980.

8   Advertisements from an agency in 1910 offered £50–£60 to professional cooks, which was the rate paid in the homes of the gentry (*IT*, 25 January 1910, p.2). Molly Keane in *Good Behaviour* described the cook, Mrs Lennon, as middle-aged, with the family for fifteen years and earning £30 a year. When she died a number of unsuccessful successors were appointed. Finally, 'after one of the undedicated cooks left without warning', the mistress offered the house/parlourmaid £1 extra to do the cooking. She then had £12 a year (pp.72, 74). This showed the big difference in pay between the specialist cook and the other servants.

9   Horn, *Rise and Fall*, p.186.

10   *Ibid.*, p.130, quoting Beeton, *Book of Household Management*.

11   Report by Miss Collet on the money wages, pp.17, 19–21, 25, 27–9.

12   Advertisements in newspapers showed that it was fairly common to give servants a rise within the first year of service. The word 'rising' appeared after the wage, or 'if satisfactory' a higher figure was mentioned. Dillon Papers: Elizabeth Dillon wages book 1896. Vere O'Brien Papers: Household account book of Robin Vere O'Brien and later, Florence Vere O'Brien 1901–22.

13   Report by Miss Collet on the money wages, p.17/25.

14   Booth, *Life and Labour*, pp.222–3.

15   B.R. Mitchell with the collaboration of Phyllis Deane, *Abstract of British Historical Statistics* (Cambridge 1962), pp.344–5.

16   *Ibid.*, pp.344–5.

17   Former butler, Co. Tipperary, to author, 27 August 1980.

18   Between 1914 and 1924 money wages generally rose by 94 per cent, but due to the rapid rise in the cost of living, real wages rose only by 11 per cent, B.R. Mitchell *et al.*, *Abstract of British Historical Statistics*, pp.344–5.

19   McBride, *Domestic Revolution*, p.60. Horn, *Rise and Fall*, p.131.

20   Report by Miss Collet on the money wages, p.10/18.

21   Advertisements in the *Drogheda Independent* in 1890 and 1902 sought general servants at £7, £9 and £12 a year, and a good plain cook at £12 a year (Drogheda Independent, 11 October 1890; 15 March 1902; also 3 January 1891 and 11 January 1892).

22   Servants were paid quarterly in all the Irish households examined; Hearn, 'Domestic Servants in Dublin'.

23   Horn, *Rise and Fall*, p.124. Charles Booth pointed out that paying weekly wages was not at all usual except with lower-class servants (Booth, *Life and Labour*, p.218),

24   Interviews with servants who worked in the 1920s and 30s.

25   Expenditure of wage-earning women and girls. Board of Trade (Labour Department). Accounts of expenditure of wage-earning women and girls, pp.28–92 [Cd 5963], HC1911, LXXXIX, 558–622. These amounts are calculated on evidence given to the above inquiry and adapted to suit Irish conditions. Rent of two rooms in Dublin was 3/- to 4/6 a week in 1912. Report of an inquiry by the Board of Trade into working class rents and retail prices in 1912, p.290/572. A girl could rent a room in the GFS Lodge in 23 South Frederick Street for 1/9 a week in 1899 (GFS Report for 1899).

In 1912 the Domestic Training Institute at 37 Charlemont Street reckoned that it cost £13 for the annual keep of a girl (GFS Minute Book 1912).

26   The GFS Minute Book for 1902-3 gives £1.4.0. a month or £14.8.0. a year as the cost of a servant's board. The cost of food for a draper's assistant who 'lived in' was £15.18.6. in 1902 (*The Draper's Assistant*, 30 August 1902).

27   Powerscourt Papers: Weekly wages analysis book of Powerscourt estate office, 1 vol., 1 September 1906-29, June 1912 (NL, Ms 19292, entries for 1 September 1906, 29 August 1908, 3 September 1910 and 29 June 1912).

28   Vere O'Brien Papers (TCD, Ms 5026, entry for 8 June 1914).

29   Report by Miss Collet on the money wages, p.10/18.

30   Hodson Papers: Account book of Sir Robert Hodson of Hollybrooke House, Kilmacanoge, Co. Wicklow, 1899-1914 (NL, Ms 16436, entries for December 1905, 1908 and 1912). Clonbrock Papers (NL, Ms 19567, entry for 12 December 1907). Dillon Papers: Private accounts 1904-7 (TCD, Ms 6721, entries for 1904, 1905, 1906). Inchiquin Papers, 1912 (NL, Ms 19569, entry 9 December 1912). Diary of Lady Charlotte Elizabeth Stopford, 1868-1911, V 20-8 (TCD, V 26, 1885-95). The entry for December 1902 records that Mary Turner got 5/-, Lucy Byrne an ulster, Andy Lawlor 2 nightshirts and port wine for his father, Mrs Matt Hudson 3 yards flannel, old clothes and tea, Mrs James, a shawl. Smith, *Irish Journals*, p.243. Margaret Powell, *Below Stairs* (London 1970), pp.85, 102, 129.

31   Vere O'Brien Papers: Personal Account Books, 1878-86 (TCD, Ms 5042, vol.1, entries for November 1882 and January 1883).

32   Clonbrock Papers (NL, Ms 19567, entries for June, July, October and November 1904, and August and December 1905).

33   Horn, *Rise and Fall*, pp.60 & 128. Frank Hugget, *Life Below Stairs* (London 1977), p.42.

34   Report of Commission on Vocational Organization in 1943 stressed that conditions largely depended on the employers, p.416.

35   Journals of the House of Commons, vol.166, 1911, no.73, Wednesday 17 May 1911; no.81, 29 May 1911, p.250. Horn, *Rise and Fall*, p.159.

36   Interviews with former servants and employers. Horn, *Rise and Fall*, p.111; Flora Thompson, *Lark Rise to Candlefort* (London 1973), p.173; Davidoff and Hawthorn, *Victorian Domestic Servant*, p.82.

37   Mary Healy, *For the Poor and for the Gentry* (Dublin 1989), pp.48 & 63.

38   L. de K.K., 'Household Hints on Furnishing Bedrooms', in *The Irish Homestead*, XI, no.45 (11 November 1905), p.833.

39   Interview with former servant at Old Folk's Association, Dún Laoghaire, on 15 October 1980. An anonymous writer said that a maid's room could be anywhere – in attic, return-room, box-room or water-tank area. An anonymous Donegal correspondent had a mere bed, worn out bed linen no floor covering, no wardrobe: 'it wasn't expected she'd have anything to put in a wardrobe'.

40   Most former servants interviewed stated that the food in service was good or very good.

41   Thompson, *Lark Rise*, p.173; McBride, *Domestic Revolution*, p.68; Katzman, *Seven Days*, p.110.

42 McBride, *Domestic Revolution*, p.68; Horn, *Rise and Fall*, p.97.

43 Former servants and employers to author.

44 Davidoff and Hawthorn, *Victorian Domestic Servant*, p.80.

45 'The Women's Parliament' in *The Lady of the House* (15 December1906), pp.15–16. One letter said: 'their hours of work are now much shorter, their outings longer'. Another: 'some years ago the class spoken of would have regarded as unobtainable luxuries the recreations and freedoms of the present time'.

46 Former servant at Terryglass, Nenagh, on 29 August 1980.

47 Former servant, Farrell Street, Kells, to author, 12 March 1980.

48 Former servant, an orphan, who worked in the west of Ireland in 1936.

49 'Holidays were never heard of' (former servant in Fennor, Slane, to author, 5 March 1980). An employer explained that she did not give her servants holidays as they generally lived nearby (former employer from Oughterard to author, 27 February 1980).

50 GFS Reports, 1884, p.5 and 1899, p.145, describe facilities provided.

51 Former servant, anonymous, to author.

52 Maids joined sodalities and so had companionship (employer in Morehampton Road to author, 26 February 1980). Servants joined the Salvation Army and sodalities for companionship (employer in Eglinton Park to author, 18 April 1980). Horn, *Rise and Fall*, p.107.

53 Report of Commission on Vocational Organization, p.417.

54 Accounts of former servants (anonymous servant, B.D.; servant from Athy to author, 2 February 1980).

55 Former servant, an orphan, who worked in the west of Ireland in 1936.

56 Former servant seen at the Dublin Central Mission, to author, 12 March 1980.

57 Hugget, *Life Below Stairs*, pp.58–9; Powell, *Below Stairs*, p.36. Former servant from Farrell Street, Kells, to author, 1 March 1980.

58 GFS Reports, 1899, p.151; 1900, p.143; 1907, p.174.

59 Booth, *Life and Labour*, p.216.

60 Former servants to author, from Kells, on 1 March 1980, and from Rotten Park, Birmingham, on 14 June 1980. McBride, *Domestic Revolution*, p.95.

61 Forty-eighth detailed annual report of the registrar general for Ireland containing a general abstract of the numbers of marriages, births and deaths registered in Ireland during the year 1911. General summary. Population, marriages, births, deaths, emigration, weather, pp.XL, XLII [Cd 6313], HC 1912–13, XIV, 52, 54.

62 *Ibid.*, XXVIII/38.

63 Lady Dilke, A. Amy Bulley, Mgt Whitley, *Women's Work* (London 1894), pp.55 & 58. Dermot Keogh, 'Michael O'Lehane and the Organization of Linen Drapers' Assistants' in *Saothar 3*, pp.36–7, described the insanitary, hazardous conditions of many of these premises in Ireland. A former servant worked in the haberdashery department of a draper's shop from 8 a.m. to 6 p.m. on four days a week, from 8 a.m. to 8 p.m. on Fridays and from 8 a.m. until the midnight tram from the Pillar reached Blackrock on Saturday.

64 Keogh, 'Michael O'Lehane', p.36.

65 Lady Dilke *et al.*, *Women's Work*, pp.50–1.

66 Keogh, 'Michael O'Lehane', p.37.
67 Deane, 'Domestic Service as a Profession', p.220.
68 Keogh, 'Michael O'Lehane', p.34.
69 R.M. Fox, *Louie Bennett*, p.68. In 1894 the average female wage in the box trade was 5/3 weekly and in match-making it was much lower (Dublin Trades Council Minutes, 11 June 1894).
70 Fox, *Louie Bennett*, pp.43, 66–70.
71 Report of Domestic Service Sub-Committee IV. Organization and conditions, 1919, p.23/29.

FOUR

1 Mark Bence Jones, *A Guide to Irish Country Houses* (London 1988), pp.xi–xxiii.
2 Elizabeth Bowen, *Bowen's Court* (London, New York & Toronto 1942), p.13.
3 Mark Girouard, *Life in the English Country House* (London 1980), p.293.
4 Ann Gregory, *Me and Nu: Childhood at Coole* (Gerrard's Cross 1970), p.33.
5 de Vere White, *The Anglo Irish*, p.173.
6 Elizabeth Bowen, *Bowen's Court and Seven Winters* (London 1984), p.281.
7 Letter from former employer in Oughterard, Co. Galway, to author, 27 February 1980.
8 Gregory, *Me and Nu*, pp.12–3.
9 Frances Cobbe, *Life of Frances Cobbe by Herself*, vol.I (2nd edn, London 1894), p.46.
10 Bowen, *Bowen's Court and Seven Winters*, extract from the Bowen Diary vol.VI, pp.326–41.
11 *Ibid.*, p.380.
12 Cobbe, *Life of Frances Cobbe*, p.47.
13 Hinkson, *Seventy Years Young*, pp.179, 209, 281, 337.
14 Former lady's maid at Nutly Park to author, 7 May 1980.
15 Employer at Oughterard to author, 27 February 1980.
16 Everett, *Bricks and Flowers*, p.28.
17 Former lady's maid at Nutly Park to author, 7 May 1980. Former butler to author, 27 August 1980. Former butler at Adare to author, 28 August 1980.
18 A former lady's maid recalled going to Dublin for the Horse Show and to attend the theatre and staying at Castletown for the Punchestown races (to author at Nutly Park on 7 May 1980).
19 Hinkson, *Seventy Years Young*, pp.121–2, 130.
20 de Vere White, *The Anglo Irish*, p.177.
21 John Ross, *Pilgrim Script* (London 1927), pp.79–80.
22 John Ross, *The Years of My Pilgrimage* (London 1924), pp.137–8.
23 Former lady's maid at Nutly Park to author, 7 May 1980.
24 The owners and frequently the whole family in 20 per cent of the enumerators' returns for country houses originally chosen were away from home. (Hearn, 'Domestic Servants in Dublin').
25 Anita Leslie, *The Gilt and the Gingerbread. An Autobiography* (London 1981), pp.81, 86.

26   Travelling expenses to London are mentioned frequently in the Clonbrock Papers: Household and general expenses books of Augusta Lady Clonbrock, 5 vols, C1903–27 (NL, Mss 19567–71).

27   Courtown Papers: Papers of the earls of Courtown on deposit in TCD Diary of Lady Charlotte Elizabeth Stopford, 1868–1911, vols 20–8 (vol.26, 1885–95).

28   Hinkson, *Seventy Years Young*, p.191.

29   Former butler, Adare Manor, to author, 28 August 1980.

30   Former butler to author, 27 August 1980.

31   David Thompson, *Woodbrook* (Harmondsworth 1977), pp.11, 13.

32   Everett, *Bricks and Flowers*, p.145.

33   Patricia Craig, *Elizabeth Bowen* (Penguin Books: 1986), pp.64, 61.

34   Everett, *Bricks and Flowers*, p.13.

35   *Ibid.*, pp.140–1.

36   E. Somerville and M. Ross, *The Big House of Inver* (London 1925), pp.10–11.

37   Cobbe, *Frances Cobbe*, p.76.

38   Nat. Arch., Cen. Ire., 1911, Antrim 140/18.

39   *Ibid.*, Monaghan 57/23.

40   *Ibid.*, Dublin 24/11.

41   Bence-Jones, *A Guide to Irish Country Houses*, pp.xiv, 267.

42   Former servant, Tara, to author, 12 April 1980.

43   Thompson, *Woodbrook*, pp.77, 78.

44   Ross, *The Years of My Pilgrimage*, p.45.

45   Inventory Book, vol.II, Oct. 1893 for Castletown House, Celbridge, by James Adam. Licensed Appraiser Auctioneer, 17 Merrion Row, Dublin.

46   Girouard, *Life in the English Country House*, p.280.

47   Robert Kerr, *The Gentleman's House* (London 1864), p.221.

48   Nat. Arch., Cen. Ire., 1911, Galway 147/12.

49   *Ibid.*, Antrim 140/18.

50   Hinkson, *Seventy Years Young*, p.115.

51   Bence-Jones, *A Guide to Irish Country Houses*, p.278.

52   Girouard, *Life in the English Country House*, p.265.

53   Craig, *Elizabeth Bowen*, p.61. According to Lady Fingall there was only one bathroom in Dublin Castle until King George's visit in 1911 (Hinkson, *Seventy Years Young*, pp.114–15).

54   Former servant at Tara to author, 12 April 1980.

55   *Ibid.*

56   Former servant to author, 29 August 1980. Former butler to author, 27 August 1980.

57   Hugget, *Life Below Stairs*, p.28.

58   Former butler, Adare Manor to author, 28 August 1980. Horn, *Rise and Fall*, p.97.

59   Booth, *Life and Labour*, p.219. Former butler to King-Harman family to author in Co. Tipperary on 27 August 1980.

60   Horn, *Rise and Fall*, p.94. Former servant from Athy to author, 2 February 1980.

61   Inchiquin Papers: Meat books of the housekeeper at Dromoland, 1877–87.

(NL Mss 14850-1).

62   J.C. Drummond & Anne Wilbraham, *The Englishman's Food* (Rev. edn., London 1957), p.430. The Irish diet was considered to have less meat than the English diet, *ibid.*, p.429.

63   The weekly consumption of meat per head for middle-class families in the 1890s in England was 3.2 lbs (Horn, *Rise and Fall*, p.96).

64   Patricia Branca, *Silent Sisterhood*, p.32. Former servant at Tara to author, 12 April 1980.

65   Merlin Waterson, *The Servants' Hall: a Domestic History of Erddig* (London 1980), p.192.

66   Former butler at Adare to author, 28 August 1980.

67   Clonbrock Papers (NL Ms 19567, 1907-9).

68   Kerr, *Gentleman's House*, p.222.

69   Inventory, Castletown House, vol.I.

70   Former servant at Nutly Park to author, 7 May 1980.

71   Kerr, *Gentleman's House*, p.279.

72   Hearn, 'Domestic Servants in Dublin'.

73   Stephen Gwynn, *Today and Tomorrow in Ireland* (Dublin 1903), pp.105, 107.

74   Everett, *Bricks and Flowers*, p.14.

75   Hearn, 'Domestic Servants in Dublin'.

76   In the same period 112 different servants were mentioned for 27 positions in the Inchiquin Papers: Wages books of domestic servants employed at Dromoland by Ethel, Lady Inchiquin, 1880-6 (NL, Mss 14848-9).

77   Clonbrock Papers: Farm, household and personal account book of Luke Gerald Dillon, 4th Baron Clonbrock, 10 vols, 1886-1917 (NL, Ms 19547, p.343), also Ms 19568, Aug. 1910.

78   Bowen, *Bowen's Court*, p.302.

79   Hinkson, *Seventy Years Young* (London 1937), p.24.

80   Bowen, *Bowen's Court*, p.13.

81   Everett, *Bricks and Flowers*, p.14.

82   Nat. Arch., Cen. Ire., 1911, enumerators' forms, Wicklow 31/21, Kildare 32/5, Down 89/9 (Hearn, 'Domestic Servants in Dublin').

83   Former servant to author at Tara on 12 April 1980.

84   Former butler to author, 27 August 1980.

85   Diary of Lady Charlotte Elizabeth Stopford 1868-1911, vols 20-8 (vol.27, 1896-1904), December 1902.

86   *Ibid.*, vol.28, December 1905.

87   Girouard, *Life in the English Country House*, p.290.

88   Clonbrock Ms 19567, 9 May 1904.

89   See Table 16, p.117; Tables 19 & 20 pp. 118-9.

90   Interview with former servant at Tara on 12 April 1980.

91   Former butler at Adare to author, 28 August 1980.

92   *Ibid.* Mrs Hunt's was mentioned in many Irish Mss. Letter to author from Massey's Agency Ltd, 100 Baker Street, on 7 October 1980, confirmed that the agency supplied staff to country houses in Ireland, especially butlers, cooks and housekeepers.

93   Others were Miss Blackwood's Office, 41 Lower Mount St; McGurrells,

32A Dawson Street.

94 Clonbrock Papers: 10 vols, 1886–1917 (NL Ms 19547), p.285; Liveries in 1890 cost £23.11.6, in 1891 £26.2.6, in 1892 £28.12.0 and in 1894 £35.1.0.

95 Former servant at Tara to author, 12 April 1980.

96 Phillis Cunnington & Catherine Lucas, *Occupational Costumes in England. From the 11th Century to 1914* (London 1976), p.182.

97 *Ibid.*, Plate 31.

98 *Ibid.*, pp.184–5.

99 Nina Slingsby Smith, *George: Memoirs of a Gentleman's Gentleman* (London 1984), p.48.

100 John Campbell Gordon, *We Twa: the Reminisences of Lord and Lady Aberdeen*, vol.ii (London 1927), pp.2–9.

FIVE

1 Report by Miss Collet on the money wages, p.25/33.

2 Clements Papers (TCD, Ms 7288).

3 Clonbrock Papers (NL, Ms 19547, p.343, also Ms 19568, Aug.1910).

4 Dillon Papers (TCD, Ms 6717).

5 Vere O'Brien Papers (TCD, Ms 5026).

6 Katzman, *Seven Days*, p.249.

7 GFS Minute book, 11 November 1886.

8 GFS Report, 1893. In 1896 a servant got a card for fifteen years service, while twenty-one got cards for periods of two to six years. (GFS Report, 1896).

9 Letter from employer in Oughterard to author, 27 February 1980.

10 Account books examined by author.

11 Letters on last month's debate – 'The Servant Difficulty – and the Way Out' – in *The Lady of the House*, VI, no.72 (15 June 1896), pp.21–2.

12 Former servant from Rotten Park, Birmingham, to author, 14 June 1980.

13 Horn, *Rise and Fall*, pp.156–9; Booth, *Life and Labour*, p.230.

14 Katzman, *Seven Days*, pp.234–5.

15 Minutes of evidence of the ITGWU to the Commission on Vocational Organization in 1940 (NL, Mss 922–41, vol.7, 928, p.2345, par. 14423). Davidoff and Hawthorn, *Victorian Domestic Servant*, p.84; Horn, *Rise and Fall*, pp.157–8; Katzman, *Seven Days*, p.234.

16 Davidoff, 'Mastered for Life: Servant and Wife in Victorian and Edwardian England' in *Society for the Study of Labour History*, Bulletin no.27 (Autumn 1973), p.24.

17 Harrison, 'For Church, Queen and Family: the GFS, 1874–1920', in *Past and Present*, nos58–61 (November 1973), no.61, p.117.

18 One servant remembered an effort to found a trade union by Louie Bennett (telephone conversation with former servant on 26 March 1980).

19 Dermot Keogh, *The Rise of the Irish Working Class: the Dublin Trade Union Movement and Labour Leadership, 1890–1914* (Belfast 1982), p.180.

20 Minutes of evidence of the IWWU to the Commission on Vocational Organization (NL, Mss 922–41, vol.4, 925, p.1309, par. 8277).

21 IWWU, Minutes of meetings, 5 November 1919–27 May 1920 (Nat. Arch., Accessions 1060/2).

22 The Domestic Workers' Union is given as a branch of the IWWU in the annual return prescribed by the registrar for a registered trade union – form A R 21 for year ending 31 December 1919. It is not mentioned on form A R 21 for 31 December 1920 (Registrar of Friendly Societies, 13 Hume Street, Dublin 2, file 332T, vol.1).

23 Evidence to the Commission on Vocational Organization, vol.4, 925, p.1310, par. 8284.

24 Ibid., vol.7, 928, p.2345, pars. 14422–3. vol.4, 925, p.1310, par. 8285.

25 Ibid., vol.9, 930, pp.3072–3, pars. 19174–9; p.3075, par. 19185.

26 Ibid., vol.4, 925, p.1310, par. 8284; p.1322, par. 8844.

27 Emmet O'Connor, 'Agrarian Unrest and the Labour Movement in County Waterford, 1917–23' in Saothar, Journal of the ILHS, 1980 (no.6), p.48.

28 Report of the Domestic Service Sub-Committee on Organization and Conditions, pp.4/10, 23/29.

29 McBride, Domestic Revolution, pp.15 & 25.

30 Beeton, Household Management, p.1518.

31 Horn, Rise and Fall, pp.118–20.

32 Ibid., p.159.

33 'What is Being Done in England. Hints for Irish Registers', from the Women's Freedom League, in The Irish Citizen, 13 July 1912, p.62; Letters from F. Sheehy Skeffington, ibid., 6 July 1912, p.53.

34 'Servants' Insurance' in The Irish Homestead, XIX, no.27 (6 July 1912), p.545.

35 Ibid. 'Servants' Insurance' in The Irish Homestead, XIX, no.26 (29 June 1912), pp.523–4.

36 Horn, Rise and Fall, p.163.

37 Former employer said she had originally opposed the 'stamp' but later paid the servant's share (to author at Eglinton Park, Dún Laoghaire, 18 April 1980).

38 'Intensifying the Domestic Servant Problem' in The Lady of the House, XX, no.221 (Christmas 1907), p.57.

39 Beeton, Household Management, p.1520.

40 Report of the Royal Commission on the Aged Poor, i, p.418 [C 7684], HC 1895, XIV, 548. McBride found considerable evidence of saving by French servants; Domestic Revolution, p.92.

41 Nat. Arch., Will book. Principal registry, 1896 A-F. Will of Mary Davis, probated 20 Jan. 1896.

42 Leslie, The Gilt and the Gingerbread, p.44.

43 Report by Miss Collet on the money wages, p.15/23.

44 Moore, Esther Waters, p.177. Servants were often given notice when they reached the age of fifty to fifty-five: 'their feet were bad and their figure gone' (former servant at Dublin Central Mission to author, 12 March 1980).

45 McBride, Domestic Revolution, p.100.

46 Horn, Rise and Fall, p.59. One of C.S. Andrews' boyhood companions was described as coming from a family which was 'the very essence of res-

pectability, his mother having been a lady's maid' (Andrews, *Dublin Made Me*, p.29).

47 Former servant in Emly to author, 16 April 1980; 'Old servants went into homes like the one in Gardiner Street, employers arranged this' (former servant in Dublin Central Mission to author, 12 March 1980).

48 There were 12,794 servants out of 55,830 inmates in 1881, 12,200 females and 594 males (Cen. Ire., 1881). There were 10,075 servants out of 42,348, in 1891, 9552 females and 523 males (Census of Ireland, 1891), i.e. 24 per cent. There was 21 per cent in 1901 and 1911 (Census of Ireland, 1901 and 1911).

49 Census of Ireland, 1881 and 1891.

50 G.D. Williams, *Dublin Charities: Being a Handbook of Dublin Philanthropic Organizations and Charities* (Dublin 1902), pp.109–19.

51 Everett, *Bricks and flowers*, p.146.

52 An employer in Roebuck had an 83-year-old servant. She was described simply as a domestic, whereas the rest had a specific position (Nat. Arch., Cen. Ire., 1911, Dublin 88/9). There was a 75-year-old ladies' maid in another household (Nat. Arch., Cen. Ire., 1911, Dublin 70/48) and a 78-year-old butler in yet another (Nat. Arch., Cen. Ire., 1911, Dublin, 86/11).

53 Mervyn Wall, *Hermitage* (Dublin 1982), p.33.

54 Nat. Arch., Cen. Ire., 1911, Antrim 140/18 and Queen's County 65/6. A retired butler in Adare Manor, who had a flat provided for him, spoke to the author, 28 August 1980.

55 *Life of Frances Cobbe by Herself*, p.36.

56 Smith, *Irish Journals*, p.114.

57 Campbell Gordon, *We Twa*, vol.1 (London 1925), pp.4–5.

58 D. O'Brien and E.W. O'Brien Papers (TCD Mss 4279–307). O'Brien, Edward William of Cahirmoyle, Co. Limerick, and Selford, Surrey. Cash book 1902–7 (Ms 4291, June 1903).

59 Powerscourt Papers: Weekly wages analysis book (NL, Ms 19292).

60 Hearn, 'Domestic Servants in Dublin'.

61 Nat. Arch., Principal registry. Will of Margery Theodora Sankey, probated 25 May 1922; will of Constantia Maria Armstrong Wilkinson, probated 2 June 1922; will of Susan Young, probated 17 August 1922; will of Kate Nolan, probated 6 December 1922.

62 One such will was that of the Rt Hon. Christopher Palles, who authorized his niece 'in her absolute discretion to pay to my servants or servants in my employment at my death and who shall have been continuously in my employment for at least five years any sum or sums but not exceeding in any case the amount of one year of their respective wages. My said niece is not to be bound to pay any sum whatever under this clause but she is to have discretion to do so if she thinks fit' (Nat. Arch., Principal registry. Will of the Rt Hon. Christopher Palles, probated 29 March 1920).

63 Some people, however, left money to former servants. Benjamin Whitaker of Avondale, Haddon Road, Clontarf, left £50 each to two sisters who were married and had left his service (Nat. Arch., Principal registry. Will of Benjamin Whitaker, probated 7 December 1922).

64 Information obtained from wills of prominent citizens and other wealthy

people. (Hearn, 'Domestic Servants in Dublin').

65 Judicial Statistics Ireland, 1879 –1900 (pp.250–1).

66 *Ibid.*, 1898. Part 1 – criminal statistics. Statistics pertaining to police, crime and its distribution – modes of procedure for punishment of crime – persons under detention in prisons and other places of confinement – for the year 1898, p.22 {Cd 225}, HC 1900, CIV, 24.

67 Nat. Arch.: Convict reference files, 1880–1919. 1880 D1-E80; '81 A1-C74; '82 D5-F28; '83 H1-K93; '84 H24-M35; '86 Mc34-S53; '88 R1-W45; '94 Mc39-S33; '96 S1-W48; '98 Mc52-V1; 1901 A1-B38; '04 D32-H20; '07 H22-M26; '10 M39-O8; '13 O2-S42; '16 S1-W21; '19 A2-C49. The 983 records were randomly selected.

68 Nat. Arch.: Convict reference files: 1880 H. Bouchier, B25; 1882 J.Ferris, F21; 1886 F. Seymour, S24; 1888 Skeen, S29; 1894 M. Sherlock, S7; 1907 H. Jackson, J8; and C. Joyce, J6; 1916 J. Sullivan, S2.

69 Judicial Statistics Ireland, 1879–1919.

70 Judicial statistics in the parliamentary papers do not record the crimes of which the prisoners were guilty. It is likely that most imprisoned domestic servants were guilty of theft.

71 Horn, *Rise and Fall*, p.133. McBride, *Domestic Revolution*, p.107.

72 Smith, *Irish Journals*, p.253.

73 Anon. employer from Donegal.

74 Horn, *Rise and Fall*, p.139. Manuscript sources record many servants discharged and, no doubt, many were discharged for dishonesty. (Clements Papers: Servants wages 1385–92 (TCD, Ms 7288; Inchiquin Papers (NL, Mss 14848–9).

75 Former employer in Kilkenny to author in the 1960s.

76 Ellen W. Darwin, 'Domestic Service' in *The Nineteenth Century*, no.CLXII, vol.28, July–December (August 1890), p.290.

77 Such an incident was described by Barbara Charlton in the following book: L.E.O. Charlton (ed.), *The Recollections of a Northumbrian Lady 1815–1866: Memoirs of Barbara Charlton Wife of William Charlton of Hesleyside, Northumberland* (London 1949), pp.215–6.

78 McBride, *Domestic Revolution*, pp.104–5.

79 Former servant to author at Nutly Park on 7 May 1980.

80 Former servant in Farrell Street, Kells, to author, 1 March 1980

81 Layton, 'Memories of Seventy Years', p.25.

82 Patrick MacGill, *The Rat Pit* (London 1915), p.183.

83 Robins, *The Lost Children*, p.154.

84 *Ibid.*

85 Three employers spoke of employing servants who had illegitimate children (at Morehampton Road on 26 February 1980; at Eglinton Park on 18 April 1980, and at Morehampton Road on 10 April 1980). Three servants had experience of working with such servants (at Emly on 16 April 1980; Farrell Street, Kells, on 1 March 1980 and anon).

86 Former servant at Nutly Park on 7 May 1980; servant from Emly on 16 April 1980.

87 Servant at Leighton Road, Crumlin on 23 March 1980.

88 Servant at Farrell Street, Kells on 1 March 1980.

89 Sean McGrath, 35 Moore Street, Kilrush, 'Patrick's Day Hiring Fair', told by Henry Greene – aged seventy-nine (Folklore Dept., UCD, Ms 1391, pp.241–2).

90 Mary Carbery, *The Farm by Lough Gur* (Cork 1973), pp.21–2.

91 GFS Reports 1879–92, p.4.

92 'Distressing Case of Suicide' in *IT*, 8 January 1883, p.6.

93 McBride, *Domestic Revolution*, p.108.

94 Poor Law Reform Commission (Ireland). Report of the vice-regal commission on poor law reform in Ireland, i, pp.42–3 {Cd 3202}, HC 1906, LI, 400–1.

95 Horn, *Rise and Fall*, pp.144–6.

96 Nat. Arch.: Confict reference file, 1888, S29. Petition of 1328, Mgt Skeen to the Lord Lieutenant of Ireland for remission of sentence.

97 'The Murder near Drogheda' in the *IT*, 10 January 1880, p.5. 'The Drogheda Murder' in the *IT*, 3 March 1880, p.2.

98 Nat. Arch.: Convict reference file, 1888, S29. Letter of the judge, the Rt Hon. GAC May to the lord lieutenant's office, 28 May 1883.

99 Nat. Arch.: Convict reference file, 1888, S29. Petition of 1328. Mgt Skeen.

SIX

1 Census of Ireland, 1871, 1881. There were 0.27 servants to each family in 1871, 0.25 in 1881.

2 GFS Report, 1901, p.26.

3 *Ibid.*, 1902, p.171.

4 *Ibid.*, 1890, p.11; 1892, p.8; 1896, p.17; 1906, p.18.

5 'The Women's Parliament' in *The Lady of the House*, VI, no.71 (15 May 1896), p.15.

6 *The Lady of the House*, VII, no.72 (15 June 1896), p.21.

7 K. Ferguson, 'The Nobility of Domestic Work' in *The Irish Homestead*, IX, no.51 (19 December 1903), p.1039.

8 Deane, 'Domestic Service as a Profession', p.219.

9 Horn, *Rise and Fall*, p.25.

10 Davidoff and Hawthorn, *Victorian Domestic Servant*, p.89.

11 'The lower classes are becoming independent preferring, when not tempted abroad by high wages, to earn their livelihood in factories and shops rather than domestic service'; typical letter in women's magazines – from Mary Rawlin in *The Lady of the House*, VII, no.72 (15 June 1896), p.21. 'Long hours standing behind a shop counter, or in noisy factories appeals *far more* to our bright, intelligent Irish girls, and all I can say is "shame". ' (K. Ferguson, 'The Nobility of Domestic Work' in *The Irish Homestead*.

12 Robert E. Kennedy, *The Irish* (Los Angeles & London 1973), p.78.

13 Approximately 25 per cent of females emigrating in the three periods 1881 to 1911 were aged fifteen to nineteen (as against 12.5 per cent for males), an average of 40 per cent were aged twenty to twenty-four and 15 per cent between twenty-four to twenty-nine. *Emigration 1948–54* (Dublin 1955), p.122.

14 Census of Ireland, 1881, 1891, 1901, 1911.

15 Census of Ireland, 1881, 1911.

16   Kennedy, *The Irish*, p.74; Katzman, *Seven Days*, pp.66-7.
17   'Irish-born servants comprised 44 per cent of all servants in 1880 in New York City and the then independent Brooklyn, 34 per cent in Philadelphia, and 19 per cent in Chicago. In Boston, Cambridge, Fall River, Hartford, Jersey City, New Haven, Province and Troy, Irish-born servants exceeded 40 per cent of all servants (Katzman, *Seven Days*, p.66). Writing of the 1920s, Kennedy showed that 81 per cent of Irish female immigrants in employment in six American states were domestic servants, *The Irish*, p.71. The 81 per cent excluded chambermaids, cooks, ladies' maids and nursemaids.
18   Kennedy, *The Irish*, p.76.
19   Daniel E. Sutherland, *Americans and their Servants: Servants in the United States from 1800 to 1920* (Baton Rouge & London 1981), p.50.
20   Hamilton, 'No Irish Need Apply', pp.7, 9, 18.
21   Royal Commission on Poor Law and Relief of Distress. Evidence of Mrs J. Ramsay McDonald, Hon. Sec. of the Legal Comittee of the Women's Industrial council, p.233 [Cd 5066], HC 1910, XLVIII, 243.
22   Kennedy, *The Irish*, p.66.
23   There was one servant in 20 of the population in 1881, this fell to one per 22 in 1891, one per 25 in 1901 and only one per 32 in 1911, Cen. Ire., 1881-1911.
24   Census of Ireland, 1926.
25   Kennedy, *The Irish*, p.67.
26   *Ibid.*, p.209. See also Irish Commission on Emigration, 1948-54, p.63.
27   Booth, *Life and labour*, p.214.
28   Royal Commission on Poor Law and Relief of Distress, p.233 [Cd 5066], HC 1910, XLVIII, 243.
29   Horn, *Rise and Fall*, p.29.
30   Crawshay, *Domestic Service for Gentlewomen*, pp.ii, 32.
31   Horn, *Rise and Fall*, p.153.
32   Margaret Huxley, 'Pursuits for Gentlewomen' in *The Lady of the House*, iii, no.5 (15 February 1893), p.8.
33   Mary Pollock, 'Pursuits for Gentlewomen' in *The Lady of the House*, iii, no.9 (15 June 1893), p.4.
34   Mary Costello, 'Dames of the Household' in *The Lady of the House*, XXI, no.229 (15 July 1908), p.8.
35   Pollock, 'Pursuits for Gentlewomen'; Letter from Mrs E. O'Neill in *The Lady of the House,* 31st year (15 November 1920), p.15. No servant in the sample taken for 'Domestic Servants in Dublin' was described as a 'lady help'.
36   Pollock, 'Pursuits for Gentlewomen', p.4.
37   Letter from Miss Caroline Emerson, 'The Women's Parliament', in *The Lady of the House*, VI, no.72 (15 June 1896), p.21.
38   'The Eight-Hour Home Assistant' in *The Lady of the House*, pp.3-4.
39   Horn, *Rise and Fall*, pp.155-6.
40   Katzman, *Seven Days*, p.127.
41   Sutherland, *Americans and their Servants*, p.195.
42   Hugget, *Life Below Stairs*, p.157.

43   'Dublin Gas Supply', Gas Company, D'Olier St, Dublin.
44   Document obtained from the Gas Company.
45   Meter Book no.32, Gas Company, Sir John Rogerson's Quay. Gas cookers were in use in Cork city about 1912. Recollections of woman who spoke to author.
46   *Dublin Electricity. The Years Before the ESB, 1881–1928* (ESB Library).
47   *City of Dublin Electricity Department, 1892–1928.* Electricity House, 39 Grafton Street (ESB Library).
48   *Dublin Electricity.*
49   'Domestic Electrification' in *City of Dublin Electricity Department.*
50   Thomas A. McLaughlin, *The Shannon Scheme Considered in its National Economic Aspect* (Sackville Press, Dublin: n.d.), pp.14–15.
51   Calder, *The Victorian Home* (London & New York 1977), p.88.
52   Manager of Nilfisk to author, 22 February 1984.
53   Norbert C. Soldon, *Women in British Trade Unions, 1874–1976* (Dublin 1978), pp.104, 144.
54   *Ibid.*, p.114.
55   Adams, *The Complete Servant*, p.13.

APPENDIX

1   Census of Ireland, 1911.
2   Untenanted lands (Ireland). Return to an order of the honourable the House of Commons, dated 27 March 1906; for a return of untenanted lands in rural districts, distinguishing demesnes on which there is a mansion, showing: (1) rural district and electoral division; (2) townland; (3) area in statute acres; (4) valuation (Poor Law); (5) names of occupiers as in valuation lists, pp 1–397, HC 1906 (250), C, 179–575.
3   Guy Routh, *Occupation and Pay in Great Britain, 1906–1960* (London 1965), p.179. The classification was based on that used in the British census of 1951.

— Index —